THE
BALTIMORE
COLTS

This scene was repeated 5,110 times during John Unitas' 17 year career in Baltimore.

Washington Redskin quarterback Eagle Day has every reason to have that pained look on his face with the likes of Gino Marchetti (89), Artie Donovan (70), Gene 'Big Daddy' Lipscomb and Ordell Braase (81) in hot pursuit.

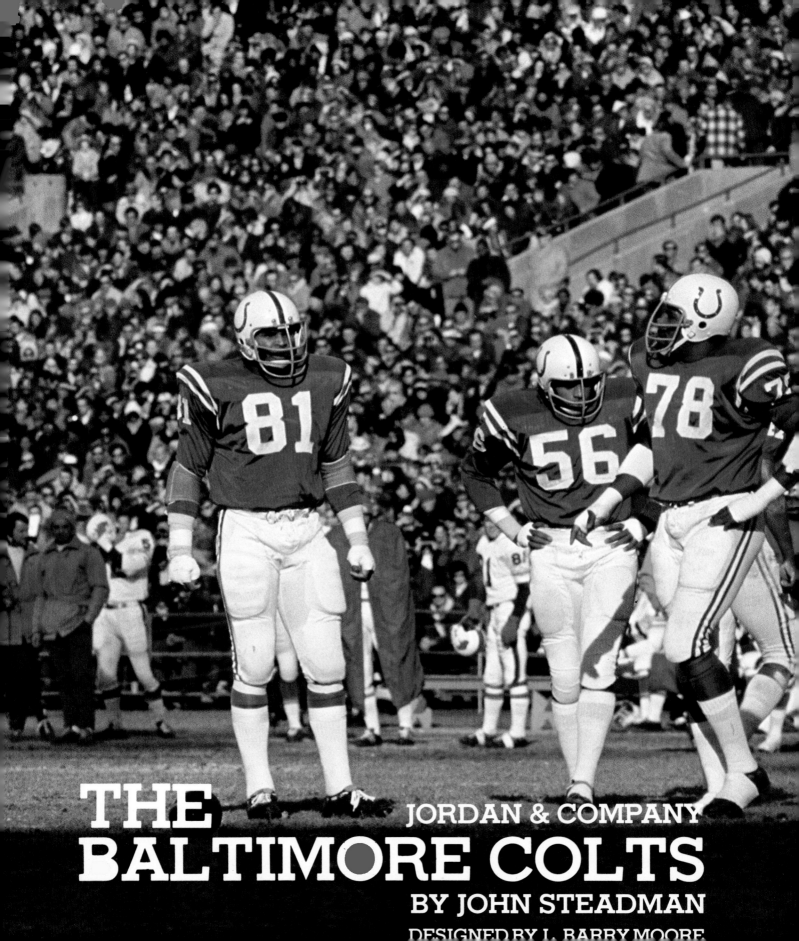

THE BALTIMORE COLTS

JORDAN & COMPANY

BY JOHN STEADMAN

DESIGNED BY J. BARRY MOORE

Library of Congress Catalogue Number LC 78-73325.

ISBN No. 0-918908-08-6.

Jordan & Company, Publishers, Inc.
1213 Laskin Road, Suite 205
Virginia Beach, Virginia 23451

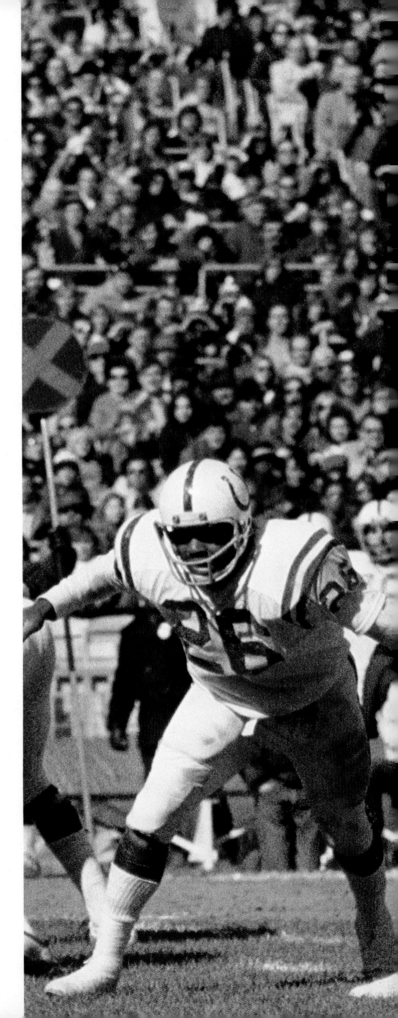

Other Titles from the Jordan & Company Sports Pictorial Series:

The Cincinnati Reds: A Pictorial History of Professional Baseball's Oldest Team.

By Ritter Collett

The Los Angeles Dodgers: The First Twenty Years.

By Frank Finch

The Pittsburgh Pirates: A Century Old Baseball Tradition.

By Richard L. Burtt

The Washington Redskins: A Pictorial History.

By David Slattery

And Also by John Steadman:

The Baltimore Colts Story.

Miracle Men of Football.

The Best (And Worst) of Steadman.

Lenny 'Spats' Moore heads around right end as Jimmy Orr provides some interference. That's middle linebacker Sam Huff of the Washington Redskins in pursuit.

To Mary Lee
Whose elegance, refinement and love
made her a winner long before
the Baltimore Colts.

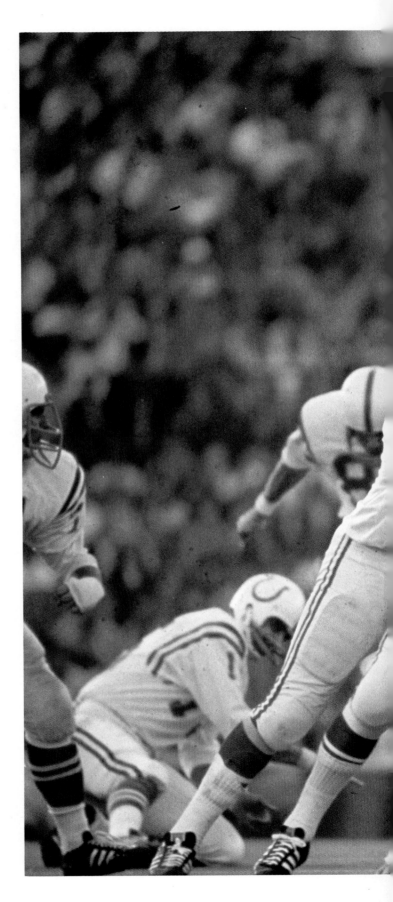

TABLE OF CONTENTS

PROLOGUE   18

CHAPTER ONE
GETTING UNDERWAY   25

CHAPTER TWO
FRANCHISE STABILITY   39

CHAPTER THREE
GREAT DISCOVERY   63

CHAPTER FOUR
TWO WORLD TITLES   71

CHAPTER FIVE
PAIN & HEARTBREAK   101

CHAPTER SIX
HORROR & HAPPINESS   121

CHAPTER SEVEN
THE TRADE   147

CHAPTER EIGHT
TRIUMPHANT TURN   155

CHAPTER NINE
FOND MEMORIES   187

INTRODUCTION

It is appropriate that a franchise with as rich a tradition as the Baltimore Colts have an up-to-date history written about it at this time. The Colts have won three World Championships, finished in first place eight times, and have won more games than any team in the National Football League since 1958.

It is also appropriate that the author of this history be John Steadman, the Sports Editor of the *Baltimore News American,* and former Public Relations Director and Assistant General Manager of the Colts. He has seen every regular season, pre-season and post-season game the Colts have ever played in the NFL. It is doubtful that any man can make that statement about any sports franchise in America. John was the Publicity Director of the Colts when I joined the team in 1956. He has always had a great feel for the Colts and a sense for their historical perspective. He is also an excellent and colorful writer. He is a personal friend of mine, and has had a deep love affair with the Baltimore Colts for 31 years. The feeling he has for the team, however, has never clouded his role as a reporter or a sports editor.

The Colts have had a proud history. Five of its players...Art Donovan, Jim Parker, Raymond Berry, Gino Marchetti, Lenny Moore...and one of its head coaches... Weeb Ewbank...are enshrined in the Professional Football Hall of Fame in Canton, Ohio. They have enjoyed championships and tasted heartbreaking defeat. But through it all, this is one of the most interesting stories in sports. It's a story of a city and its love for a football team. And there is no better man to tell that story than John Steadman.

John Unitas

October 3, 1978.

PROLOGUE

Some professional football franchises have been in existence for decades of frustration and failure and are still in search of a quarterback who could lead them to the hopeful "promised land" of touchdowns and championships. The Baltimore Colts are a notable exception, a striking example of good fortune, like finding a pearl in a Chesapeake Bay oyster. Not once but three times. They don't have those horseshoes on their helmets for nothing. That's the inevitable deduction you arrive at in any study of how the Colts have ridden along "happy trails" to continuing success.

Three extraordinary quarterbacks, endowed with exceptional arms, have come to the Colts by a most unusual thread of circumstance. More by luck than design. The first one, Y.A. Tittle, was an outright gift from the Cleveland Browns, who were made to feel sorry for the team's sad state of affairs in 1948 and actually handed him over in an effort to help the Colts improve themselves.

The presence of Tittle immediately took the Colts to a position of respectability — a tie for the Eastern Division of the All-America Conference. He was only 21 years old and a picture passer with a fluid, effortless delivery.

Then the Colts hit the jackpot a second time and got the most famous quarterback of them all, John Unitas, the near-peerless performer at this most exacting position the game has ever known. He was a "find", a free-agent who had been turned out by his own hometown Pittsburgh Steelers, who didn't think enough of his talents to allow him to participate in a single play of even a meaningless exhibition game in 1955. It was the mistake of the age, costing Pittsburgh dearly, but a windfall for Baltimore.

Unitas, the reject, was to take the Colts to successive world championships in 1958 and 1959 and set personal and team records, plus gaining rich respect from the public, press and, more importantly, players on both sides of the scrimmage line.

Tittle didn't cost anything and neither did Unitas. How lucky could one team be? Then "along came Jones", as the lyrics in the song relate, first name Bert. He, like Tittle and Unitas, was the result of a team not realizing what it could have.

Jones was born and raised in Ruston, Louisiana, the backyard of the New Orleans Saints, but was passed over. The Saints owned the draft choice that could have brought them Jones in 1973. They elected, however, to trade the pick for a journeyman defensive tackle named Billy Newsome and the Colts' fourth round selection, who turned out to be Jim Merlo, of Stanford, who became a respectable linebacker.

Here's Y.A. Tittle (left) when he was a campus hero at LSU and then as a rookie sensation with the Colts. Tittle was virtually the team's entire offense in Baltimore from 1948 through 1950.

The Colts can take all the bows they want, over landing Jones, including everlasting credit to then general manager Joe Thomas, who made this "steal of a deal", but the fact remains it never would have happened without the cooperation at the time of the Saints' head coach, J.D. Roberts.

It was the Saints' belief, specifically Roberts, that the young QB they had drafted two years earlier, Archie Manning of Mississippi, had the capabilities to make them a contender and they didn't need

Jones, whose father had played at Tulane University in New Orleans, had later been a standout with the Cleveland Browns and was well-known all over Louisiana.

Young Bert had set 20 passing marks at LSU that virtually forced them to rewrite the record book. But, in the opinion of the Saints, the homegrown product didn't figure in their plans, much to their subsequent regret.

The Colts took advantage of the Saints lack of belief in Jones' potential and their over-estimation of what Manning would do. And — get this — the Saints sought out the Colts to make the trade. They asked for it and Thomas obliged.

A very young Y.A. Tittle confers with head coach Cecil Isbell on the sidelines during a game against the Chicago Rockets on Sept. 10, 1948. Tittle came to the Colts as a "gift" from the Cleveland Browns.

This is how John Unitas looked shortly before he was released from the Pittsburgh Steelers in 1955.

Peter Finney, sports editor of *The New Orleans States Item*, told this writer that Roberts initiated the transaction with the Colts. And Harry Hulmes, a former general manager of the Colts who joined the Saints organization in 1970, said to the best of his recollections that was how the trade originated. Hulmes is more willing to agree than to disagree that Finney's version is correct.

Roberts was fired as the Saints' coach before the next season even started. If he had selected Jones and dealt off Manning, or even kept both, the Saints' fortunes may have taken a far different turn. New Orleans has had to accept continuing embarrassment over the loss of Jones, the same as Pittsburgh suffered the humiliation of having Unitas in its training camp and being unable to recognize a future Hall of Fame talent. The fact the Saints were receptive to give the Colts a chance to talk to them about acquiring their first round pick was a total surprise.

And Thomas wasn't about to stand around counting the flowers on the wall when he heard the Saints were interested in dealing off their No. 1 choice for the likes of Newsome and a college draft choice in the fourth round.

Thomas was elated when the Houston Oilers, drafting first, elected to take end-tackle John Matuszak from the University of Tampa. Joe could hardly restrain himself at the thought of getting

Jones. Minutes after taking the LSU product, he exclaimed he had gotten an exceptional prospect, the type of a passer who only comes along about as often as the 17 year locusts.

Jones brought with him a strong body, 6-foot-3, 205 pounds, a powerful arm that could put the ball in the air long distances, agility, speed afoot and durability. He was a well coordinated and competitive athlete with style and poise to go with his immense ability.

Ironically, the Cleveland Browns had Jones in their camp when he was only a junior high school student. He came there to be with his father, Dub Jones, who was then an assistant coach for the Browns. Bert spent his time chasing loose footballs on the practice field and helping equipment manager Morrie Kono and trainer Leo Murphy with locker room chores.

The Browns desired to make the Colts an offer for Jones but Thomas wasn't at all interested. And, continuing on with the Baltimore-Cleveland quarterback connection, the Browns also wanted Unitas in their camp for 1956 but the Colts signed him before they could make a move.

It's a part of history that when Unitas was released by the Steelers in 1955, he sent the Browns a telegram telling them of his availability but their roster was set and Otto Graham, a subsequent Hall of Famer, was in control. They didn't need a quarterback right then but hoped to take a look at him the following year. It didn't figure, under any condition, that Unitas, cut by the Steelers, would be in demand.

Stop to think of the success that would have come about in Cleveland if Unitas had gone to the Browns instead of the Colts and been standing-by to succeed Graham when he retired after the 1955 season.

The reason the Colts got Tittle from the Browns in 1948 was because coach-general manager Paul Brown realized that in Graham he had the best QB in pro football at the time. The only possible way Tittle was going to get to play was if Graham happened to break both legs, which was highly unlikely considering the way the Browns protected him with their pass blocking.

But by placing Tittle in Baltimore, in the days when the All-America Conference was struggling to stay in existence, meant the Colts could be competitive and be more than a facsimile of a football team. Brown gave him to the Colts for the overall good of keeping the All-America Conference operating and assisting a club that needed an infusion of personnel.

Y.A. was with the Colts in 1948, '49 and '50 and went back into the draft when the Baltimore franchise was illegally forfeited by the National

20

Fullback Bus Mertes rips off a five-yard gain for the Colts against the Buffalo Bills in 1948. This was the controversial playoff game where an official decision influenced the outcome and Baltimore fans stormed the field when it was over.

What the well-dressed Colts wore in 1948, when they were out of football togs, is typified by Lu Gambino (left) and Sam Vacanti as they're pictured in downtown Baltimore. The Colts signed Gambino after he was declared ineligible for further play at Maryland as the result of a highly controversial ruling.

piece of football merchandise and to take him. He did.

The Baltimore group of owners, led by the tenacious Krieger, Embry, Hilgenberg, Mullan, Howard Busick and Vic Skruck, plus the 202 stock holders, were furious over Watner's action. They felt they had been robbed and insisted Watner had no more legal right to sell or give the franchise to the league than they had to peddle Fort McHenry. They instituted legal moves and engaged William D. Macmillan, Sr., to handle the case. Macmillan was an astute attorney, glib, colorful and able to engage in give-and-take, offense and defense, depending upon the strategy needed.

Most of the information Macmillan used was gathered from a scrapbook of newspaper clippings John Sanborne, the equipment manager, had kept on a daily basis, sometimes buying two and three editions of the same day's paper. Macmillan and Bell hit it off on a friendly personal note, even though they were on rival sides. They were similar in their physical builds, short and blocky, and both had a sense of humor that was an appealing part of their personalities.

Macmillan made it clear to Bell and the league counsel that Baltimore didn't want a financial settlement in the dispute. What it was after was restoration of the team. The league realized, after Chief Judge W. Conwell Smith ruled in Baltimore's favor during a hearing on the motions, that it was in deep trouble and left it to Bell to find the best solution possible. This meant that Bell had to provide Baltimore with a team, which is what Macmillan had been asking.

It came to pass that the Dallas Texans' club, which had moved from New York at the start of the 1952 season, got little support at the box-office. The owners there were Giles and Connell Miller. Dallas didn't respond to pro football the way the league anticipated and after three home games, the Texans, under-financed, were taken over by the NFL. They completed the rest of the schedule on the road and its bills were paid by the League.

A whimsical Irishman named James Michael Phelan, with a personality that was most engaging, was the coach of the Texans. He fortunately never made the mistake of taking himself or the team too seriously. On one occasion after they had received their pay, Phelan gathered the assistant coaches and players around him. He said, "Boys, I'm not saying these checks aren't any good, but take one lap around the field and run for the bank."

Phelan, another time, on Thanksgiving Day, when the Texans were preparing to play and win their only game, against the Chicago Bears in the Rubber Bowl at Akron, got up in the locker room, and commented wryly: "There are so few spectators today we are going to dispense with the formal introductions and go up in the stands and meet everybody personally."

The Texans had better talent than the record of 1 and 11 showed but they needed a quarterback. Put a Tittle or a Burk with what the Texans had and you may have had a contender. But, unfortunately, the Colts of 1950 had been dismantled and Tittle was in San Francisco and Burk in Philadelphia.

Two former players were to return, however, namely Donovan and Averno. Donovan and Averno had been with the Browns in 1951, were sent to the Yanks in trades and then on to the Texans. They had come full cycle in only three years.

Now that the promise to put a team back in Baltimore had been fulfilled, Bell had to find a way to finance it. He gave the city a challenge. He said the Texans' players assets would be given to Baltimore if the public would buy 15,000 season tickets, paid in full, not pledges, in a six-week time span over the Christmas holiday season of 1952.

It was a happy locker room scene for Billy Hillenbrand, coach Cecil Isbell and Y.A. Tittle with the 1948 Colts. Hillenbrand was an exceptional broken-field runner and Tittle had one of the strongest and most accurate passing arms football has ever known. Isbell, before he coached the Colts, was an outstanding player for the Green Bay Packers and was the throwing part of the famed "Isbell to Don Hutson" combination.

A consistant performer at offensive guard and tackle during the late 1940's was Barry French, a product of Purdue University.

Academy. So Molesworth was well-known in the area and a highly popular choice.

For general manager, Bell brought up the name of Don Kellett, like Rosenbloom, a former Penn athlete. One strong reason Bell considered Kellett was because only the season before, when the Texas team was suffering, Kellett had gone to him with a most unusual and intriguing proposition. It was Kellett's idea the Texans could be called the "All-Americans", put on tour and play out of a different city each week. The games would be televised on the Dumont Network, preferably Saturday nights, which was the purpose of Kellett's proposal.

But Bell told him there were other plans for the Texans. As it worked out, he was able to turn the Dallas problem into a plus, switching the club to Baltimore where the suit would be negated. That was precisely the way it evolved and the setting was arranged for what eventually turned out to be the most successful and exciting phase of football emotionalism any city has ever enjoyed.

Baltimore more than succeeded the goal. Bruce Livie, a Baltimore auto dealer, who had once thought of buying a team for the city when the All-America Conference was starting, was asked to lend his name to chairmanship of the ticket drive. He did and, ultimately, became a part owner of the new club.

Embry, Krieger, Hilgenberg and Mullan, all leaders of the group that had battled to have the Colts returned, didn't want any part of operating the new team even though there was $300,000 in capital from the sale of season tickets. They reminded Bell he had agreed to find an owner. Where was his man?

Bell believed he could induce Carroll Rosenbloom, a Baltimorean who had played halfback at the University of Pennsylvania, to become the owner. Bell vacationed in Margate, N.J., and was a neighbor of Rosenbloom, who was living there. It took some convincing but Bell managed to do it.

Before that, Bell told Rosenbloom he had a likely coach and general manager available. The coach was Keith Molesworth, who had played halfback for the Chicago Bears and had also been a shortstop for the Baltimore Orioles of the International League, plus a coach at the Naval

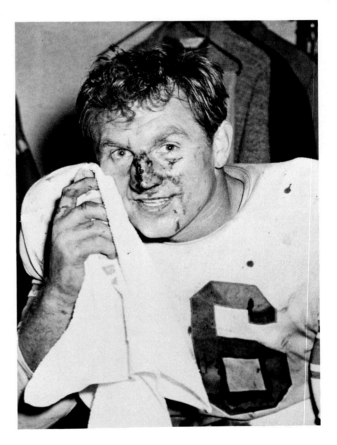

All for love of the game. That's Zollie Toth, fullback, putting a cold towel to the side of his bruised and bleeding face after an afternoon of football battle. Toth suffered a broken nose but never missed a play.

34

Maybe a rolling stone doesn't gather much moss, as the cliche reminds, but here's a Stone, first named Billy, gaining long yardage with a kickoff return against the New York Yanks. Stone is getting convoy assistance from Wendell Williams (No. 53) and Paul Page (No. 88). The Yankee being taken out of the way is Len (Tuffy) McCormick (No. 26), who had played for the Colts the year before, 1948.

Quarterback Y.A. Tittle greets Bob Williams, a Baltimore product, during a visit to training camp. This was the summer of 1949, as Williams prepared for his junior year at Notre Dame and All-America recognition. Williams later came to the Colts in a trade from the Chicago Bears but was called to military service and never got a chance to play for his hometown team.

36

President Harry S. Truman is presented a season pass to all the Colts' games in 1949 but never had a chance to use it because he was too busy running the country — even on Sunday afternoons in the fall. Making the presentation at the White House are (left to right) R.C. (Jake) Embry, Colts' president; Commodore O.O. Kessing, commissioner of the All-America Conference, and Walter Driskill, general manager of the Colts.

The man holding for the kicker is Herman Wedemeyer, who played for the Colts in 1949 before playing in "Hawaii Five-0" and other TV productions. "Hula Hips Herman", as he was dubbed, is shown after placing the ball in a kicking drill with Rex Grossman.

One of the most popular Colts ever was linebacker-defensive end Bob Nowaskey, showing here why he was considered one of the most awesome tacklers in Baltimore's history. His victim here is future Colts standout George Taliaferro who played for the Los Angeles Dons at the time this photo was taken in 1949 and came to the Colts when the Dallas franchise was moved to Baltimore in 1953.

"The Gladiator". Art Donovan, jacket draped across his shoulders, and helmet under his arm, awaits the moment to respond for defensive duty. Donovan was the first Colt to be voted into the Hall of Fame and was so highly respected by rival teams that they frequently refused to even try his side of the line.

CHAPTER TWO
FRANCHISE STABILITY

It's regarded in retrospect as a positive development in the love story of a football team and a city. The fact the Colts were summarily discharged by the NFL at the end of the nightmarish campaign of 1950 brought resentment. Watner, the ex-president, had his house "bombed" with obscene words and exploding firecrackers. The league had no right to take away the Colts, acting capriciously and without regard to the legal ownership.

This led to a desire by the citizenry to tell itself it would show the NFL what a huge mistake it had made. The Colts, thanks to the fans, returned from the dead, so to speak, and not only became a viable part of pro football but won championships and emerged as a symbol of pro football affluence and affection. The Colts were to stand tall as an effective advertisement for not only themselves but the entire league.

Baltimore had a desire to have a team and the locale made it a perfect setting. World War II, when Baltimore became an immense industrial hub and was seemingly surrounded by military installations, brought vast population increases to the city. Workers and servicemen from West Virginia, Pennsylvania, Tennessee, Virginia, North and South Carolina decided to stay and take up permanent residency. They liked the old city and its charm.

A pro franchise gave one and all a means of identification. Baltimore didn't have a major college football team, only Johns Hopkins University, where the sport was low-key. The University of Maryland was on the rise but it never actually captured the rooting interest of Baltimore, despite the fact there were such outstanding area products playing there as Jack Scarbath, Elmer Wingate, Jack Targarona and Dick Bielski.

So pro football had a metropolitan market all unto itself. It wasn't like Los Angeles, where the Rams had to cope with Southern California and UCLA, or Chicago, where Northwestern, Purdue, Illinois and Notre Dame had strong alumni, both bonafide and self-proclaimed.

In Baltimore, the Colts reigned. They were back in harness. It was 1953. A rebirth. To save money, the team merely transferred the colors of the Dallas Texans, blue, white and silver, and officially adopted same. There was a brief desire at the outset to junk the old name and not call them the Colts.

But a young sports writer from *The News American* got on his feet at a meeting held in the tap-room of the Gunther Brewery and, before a group of city officials, said the Colts' name should never be

Clem Crowe (left), a former Notre Dame end under the legendary Knute Rockne, is given a handshake and a two year contract from club president Abe Watner in 1950.

eliminated. Besides, it would be giving in to the NFL in its subtle desire to rub out Baltimore's football past. Another sports writer, James Ellis, of *The Evening Sun* seconded the motion.

Even the sideline coats of the Texans were utilized by having a tailor put patches over the former name. Baltimore's uniforms in the All America Conference had been a dull green and silver, a poor combination, so almost any switch would have been for the better.

The team song, "Fight On You Baltimore Colts", which had been written in 1947, was another link with the past that was important. In fact, years later, a nationally known authority on music said the Colts' song was one of the finest in the country, from both a playing and listening standpoint. The words and music were by Jo Lombardi and Benjamin Klasmer, assisted by Tommy Dukehart, who was the club's first publilcity man.

The Colts' band was always ready to go. It had never broken ranks during the two years the team was out of business. Bob Cissin, then the director, kept the group together and had it perform at parades and civic gatherings, the only band in the land representing a nonexistent football team. So things were ready for the re-entry of Baltimore to the NFL. There was even a group of businessmen called the "Colts Associates". They concentrated on helping with promotions and getting the players acclimated.

Players from the Texans were to come to Baltimore, including Averno, Donovan, Colo, Claude (Buddy) Young, George Taliaferro, Gino Marchetti, Tom Keane, Dan Edwards, Alex Agase, Ken Jackson, Frank Tripucka, Bob Celeri, Ray Pelfrey and Jim Mutscheller, who was on the reserve list of the Texans because he had been off fighting a scrimmage with live ammunition as a Marine Lieutenant in Korea.

The Colts also took part in the 1953 college draft. Billy Vessels, the Heisman Trophy winner from Oklahoma, was their first pick but preferred, instead, to sign with the Edmonton Eskimos of the Canadian League. He had a highly produtive year at Edmonton and was voted the outstanding player in the Dominion. Tripucka and Celeri also went to Canada, leaving the Colts without a skilled quarterback.

They picked up Fred Enke from the Philadelphia Eagles. He was mechanically a good QB but lacked fire-power. Still later that season, Enke suffered a shoulder separation and his loss was felt.

Kellett was the general manager and Molesworth the coach. Odd, but Kellett and Molesworth had been baseball teammates at second base and short-stop when they played briefly at Syracuse in the International League. Kellett remembered meeting Rosenbloom at a University of Pennsylvania alumni

function but didn't get to know him on a personal basis until he started working for him.

The general manager's role fit Kellett. He had an extensive background, having been an athlete and coach at Penn and later a radio-television executive at station WFIL in Philadelphia. He was an able public speaker, a well-disciplined executive who made every moment count and had a way with people that found him gaining popularity and respect. Rosenbloom gave him full latitude in the job but, Kellet, in return also provided loyalty and a high degree of professionalism.

At the end of the first year, there was a clause in Kellett's contract that meant he could buy into ownership but he withdrew the option. He later regretted doing that and said his mother told him it was a poor decision for him to make. Rosenbloom held 51 percent of the ownership and the other 49 belonged to Hilgenberg, Mullan, Krieger, and Livie.

A case of a wrong caption, which happens on the best of newspapers. This picture labeled Art Donovan as the player throwing a block that springs John Huzvar to the outside in the opening 1953 win over the Chicago Bears. Actually, the block is being delivered by Joe Campanella. Number 17 for the Colts is quarterback Fred Enke. The Colts won, 23-17, to score a major upset. Donovan, who was never in a single offensive play, loves this picture.

In 1950, the Colts had Eddie King as middle guard. He later distinguished himself as director of the Massachusetts Port Authority and won the Democratic Party's nomination as governor of the state . . .the first time any former major league athlete had ever tried for a governorship.

This is the way the Colts looked up front, in 1953, when pro football returned to Baltimore after a two year lapse. In the front, left to right, are Barney Poole, Tom Finnin, Sisto Averno, Art Donovan and Art Spinney. The linebackers are Alex Agase, later to be head coach at Northwestern and Purdue, and Ed Sharkey.

The league stipulated the initial payment for the franchise would have Rosenbloom put up $13,000, and Hilgenberg, Mullan, Krieger and Livie $3,000 each for a total of $25,000. There was $300,000 in funds raised from the ticket sales so the franchise from that point on would be self-sustaining.

The 1953 team was augmented by a ten-for-five player deal Kellett arranged with Paul Brown. The Colts dealt away Colo, Mike McCormick, Hershel Forrester, John Petibon and Tom Catlin for Bert Rechichar, Art Spinney, Carl Taseff, Don Shula, Stu Sheetz, Elmer Willhoite, Dick Batten, Gern Nagler, Ed Sharkey and Harry Agganis, who had been a high Cleveland draft pick as a quarterback but

signed, instead with the Boston Red Sox as a first baseman.

It's a little known fact that Agganis, while he was with the Red Sox, was considering coming to the Colts. He was later to be taken ill and died at the premature age of 25 in 1955.

Oddly enough, in 1956, the Colts went on to play an exhibition in Boston with the New York Giants for the Harry Agganis Memorial Fund, the first game Unitas ever started as a pro. But in 1953 they didn't have Agganis and they had never heard of Unitas. They had to do with Enke, Jack Delbello, Dick Flowers and Ed Mioduszewski (Meadows) as their quarterbacks. And there was even an occasion

It was a historic meeting when Commissioner Bert Bell visited Baltimore in December of 1952 and met with the board of directors of the former Colts' franchise. In the picture are (left to right) R.C. (Jake) Embry, Tom Mullan, Commissioner Bell, Zanvyl Krieger, Bill Hilgenberg (rear), attorney William Macmillan and Howard Busick. It was on this occasion that Bell said 15,000 season tickets had to be sold for Baltimore to get the franchise of the defunct Dallas Texans.

42

against the Rams when Taliaferro played the position and looked good.

The Colts won three games, including the opener against the Chicago Bears when Rechichar pounded home a then world record field goal of 56 yards. It was kicked on a low trajectory, a line drive, and had so much velocity to it that it carried beyond the back line of the end zone.

The arrival of Young and Taliaferro meant Baltimore was going to have Black players for the first time in football. Young, without question, played an important role in breaking down much of the racial prejudice that existed. He was voted the team's most popular player in a poll of the fans, which signified that Baltimore, a city which historians tell us had decided Southern leanings during the Civil War, was changing socially.

The impression was drawn that Rosenbloom, who was a business tycoon, started off only mildly interested in the Colts, but, as the season progressed, became avid. There were times when he accompanied Kellett to the bench area and mingled with the players while the game was in progress. But they didn't interfere and the only year he was observed there was in 1953.

Rosenbloom was deeply impressed with the effort put forth by the squad and realized the coaching had to be up-graded. It was decided Molesworth would become the personnel director. Not all teams had a player talent coordinator at that point in time but it was a position where he could be placed that wouldn't be at all embarrasing to a highly admired individual. The Colts' first attempt to get a coach was rebuffed by the Cleveland Browns. The man they preferred was Blanton Collier, defensive backfield aide, but he said he wasn't interested.

A member of the Browns' board of directors told Rosenbloom the individual who would do the best job for the Colts wasn't Collier but Wilbur (Weeb) Ewbank, who was the tackle coach and also in charge of preparing the Browns' draft lists. Brown was reluctant to let Ewbank leave and was most unhappy when Weeb showed up late at the Senior Bowl game, where both were coaching. He was being interviewed by Kellett for the Baltimore position, which annoyed Brown. He was more upset in the weeks to come.

When Ewbank took the post, Brown insisted he not be allowed to station himself at the Colts' table at the draft. But Ewbank slipped information to the Colts anyhow and that's how Raymond Berry of SMU was drafted on the 20th round as a future.

Ewbank brought quick stability to the Colts on the field. What Brown developed in Cleveland was now the Baltimore system. There were team meetings preceeding every workout, a film grading of players on a game-by-game basis and what amounted to a highly professional approach in all matters. It was

evident from the first day at Western Maryland College. That was when Ewbank informed the players at training camp there was no "magic carpet" method to earn a championship, only concentration and application.

In 1953, the Colts had an "incentive plan" where they got $10 and other monetary rewards for things like blocking kicks, intercepting passes, recovering fumbles, etc., but Ewbank decided against that. Rosenbloom had, however, cut the players and coaches in for some of the profits following the 1953 season and continued the practice until the league made him stop. It was, naturally, the most popular policy he ever instituted. The team realized it was going to get a bonus at the end of the year if the organization had a good year at the box-office. Like $300 or $500 a man.

Coach Keith Molesworth, left, meets his 1953 coaching staff, Nick Wasylik., Ray Richards and Otis Douglas, seated, who also served as team trainer. Molesworth had been a shortstop for the Baltimore Orioles in the International League and was later a coach at the Naval Academy. He also was the Colts' first personnel director.

Pursued by an unfriendly Washington Redskin, George Taliaferro is about to be pushed out of bounds in this game at Memorial Stadium in 1953. Taliaferro could run, punt and pass and even served as an emergency quarterback on one occasion.

The move also brought favorable reaction in the press around the country and impressionable college players, reading about the generous action of Rosenbloom, weren't at all dismayed when they learned they were drafted by the Colts. Suddenly, what was the "pits" of football became a highly pleasurable place to be. The Colts were regarded as a team on the rise.

It developed that the Colts had a couple of new things going for them in 1954 . . .horseshoe designs on their helmets, an idea presented by publicitor Sam Banks, and the organization of the first successful cheer-leading unit, headed by Mrs. Thelma Mack. The well-received Colts' Corralls, a fan club concept, came later at the suggestion of Leo Novak, a plumber, and Ed Loud, a dog food salesman.

The 1954 exhibitions found the Colts making an excellent impression. Ewbank's well orchestrated operation was coming along beautifully. Then the season opened. What a contrast. It was sudden disaster, a 48-0 beating by the Los Angeles Rams in Baltimore. The Rams scored on the first play, following the opening kickoff, when they used the old "sleeper" act by having Volney (Skeets) Quinlan station himself near the Rams' bench and not even visit the huddle. Quarterback Norm Van Brocklin merely faded back and arched a pass down the east sidelines to Quinlan for an 80-yard touchdown that opened the gates.

As the season progressed, the Colts looked the part of a stronger team even though their record was no better than the previous year, 3 and 9. They were improved, even if it didn't show in the standings but it was apparant help was needed.

As the Colts were completing the schedule on the West Coast in mid-December, Ewbank decided it would be beneficial if the team could scout the all-star and bowl games that were soon to be played there. Molesworth, meanwhile, had established a scouting system, where assistant coaches on college teams were asked to file a report on players in their conference. The pay was $50 for the year, which was the standard fee paid by most clubs, plus Rosenbloom sent each of the scouts gift sports shirts from his Marlboro factory as a personal touch.

As to covering the bowl game practices, the decision about what to do was resolved when Ewbank looked at his coaching staff and said the only bachelor who didn't have to be home for the Christmas season was line coach Joe Thomas. If he had been married with a family there's no way to tell what would have happened. So Thomas was told to remain in California and watch the various workouts of the college teams near Los Angeles and San Francisco. From this informal beginning, Thomas was ultimately to gain stature as one of the

Hemlines and hair styles were somewhat different in 1953 when this picture was taken of Sallie Possell, "Miss Colt", and the team's mascot, "Dixie", who was present for all the games and circled the field any time the team scored.

most capable appraisers of football talent. But that's where it all started.

That year, going into the draft, the Colts were prepared to make Larry Morris, a linebacker from Georgia Tech, as their No. 1 pick. But the night before the selection system commenced, Ewbank, Molesworth, Kellett, Rosenbloom and the assistant coaches were huddled in a meeting at the Hotel Warwick in New York. It was Thomas who spoke out and made a strong plea to the group that it focus its attention on getting offensive players, rather than Morris, a linebacker, because the Colts had adequate defense.

Thomas' logic impressed Rosenbloom enough that the thinking was changed. The entire philosophy was altered at the "eleventh hour". The Colts were going to be trying to get prospects with offensive capabilities. The Colts also got lucky. They won the bonus choice, a flip of the coin, that proceeded the draft proper.

This gave them the chance to call the name of any college product in the country. They decided on George Shaw, quarterback, Oregon, and then named Alan (The Horse) Ameche, the Heisman Trophy winner of Wisconsin, as their regular first round selection. Subsequently, they gathered such blue-chip prospects as L.G. (Long Gone) Dupre of Baylor, Dick Szymanski of Notre Dame, George Preas of VPI and Jack Patera of Oregon. In all, 12 rookies made the squad.

It became a star-spangled array, one of the most productive drafts any team ever had. It was a group

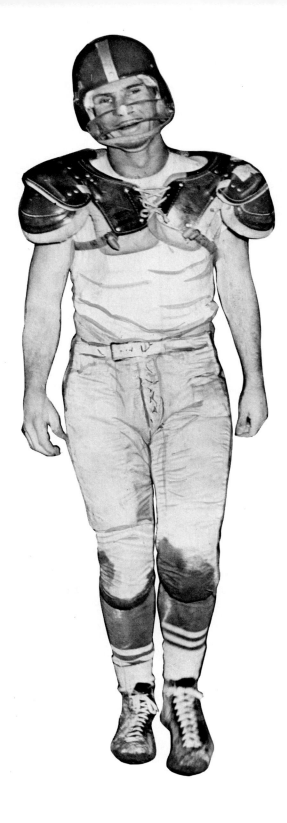

long on ability and a desire to play. The Colts opened against the Bears and, like sudden thunder booming, Ameche exploded for 79 yards on the first play from scrimmage. It was a smart coaching plan by Ewbank that made it happen. The Colts had noticed in watching films of the Bears that tackle John Kreamcheck would "key" off a pulling guard and follow him to the ball carrier, or where the play was being directed.

But the Colts intentionally "suckered" the Bears. Alex Sandusky pulled out of the line, leaving a wide hole, Kreamcheck took the bait and Ameche went through the area he vacated, storming, untouched, for the touchdown. The Colts went on to win another upset. Hopes were high and improvement in all areas was apparent. The Colts were a team that was going to merit respect and, possibly, be a contender in the none too distant future.

Donald S. (Red) Kellett is regarded as one of the finest administrators any Baltimore sports team ever had. He was a three-sport standout at Penn, a graduate of the Wharton School of Finance and an articulate public speaker. Kellett was general manager from 1953 through 1966.

When Y.A. Tittle returned to Baltimore in 1953 with the San Francisco 49ers, his team won the game but Y.A. lost his shirt. That's right, the Tittle admirers literally tore the jersey right off his back. Police officers had to rescue Y.A. from the fans. Y.A.'s comment: "Look here, boy, didn't I tell you how gracious these Baltimore fans are?"

The 1956 season was marked with building enthusiasm. The draft of Lenny Moore on the first round was hailed as a plus. But Dick Donlin, the second pick from Hamline, was a poor choice. The third round selection was Bob Pascal of Duke, a strong runner, but he, like Vessels two years before, signed with the Canadian League, specifically the Montreal Alouettes. Yes, this is the same Bob Pascal who later became the chief executive of Anne Arundel County and a possible future candidate for Governor of Maryland.

The Colts were putting together a team with the highest of hopes. They had the two leading rookies of 1955, Shaw and Ameche, to go with Moore, the top rookie of 1956, in the backfield. And then they signed Vessels, a player the Rams had once offered an entire team, eleven (11) men, if they could only have his draft rights. But Vessels, after one year in Canada and two in the service, returned to join the Colts amid trumpets and fanfare.

Ewbank learned about it from Kellett and Rosenbloom. The negotiations were handled by

Rosenbloom and Vessels wanted to come to the National League and join this team that had so much promise. Ewbank for some reason, seemed to resent Vessels and played him only spasmodically but the strong runner from Oklahoma, who Szymanski to this day says is the greatest natural talent he ever saw, injured himself early in training camp. When he did return, Vessels played on special teams. Late in the season, with injuries hampering the Colts, he started against the Redskins and Rams. Vessels more than acquitted himself, gaining in excess of 100-yards and blistering the goal-line.

The season of 1956, however, was to be his first and last one in Baltimore. He felt it wasn't worth subjecting himself or his family to controversy. He retired from the Colts at age 25, went with the Mackle Corp., in Florida and never uttered an unkind word about Ewbank. He forgot the past.

That season of 1956 was to bring the remarkable discovery of an immense individual football talent, so not all was lost.

This was the start of Weeb Ewbank's successful career as a head coach, which led him to eventual selection in the Pro Football Hall of Fame. Ewbank flashes a smile and a contract on the day in 1954 when he was named coach of the Colts. With him is general manager Don Kellett.

This was the first time the group which led the fight to have Baltimore returned to pro football met with the new controlling owner, Carroll Rosenbloom. Surrounding Rosenbloom are (left to right) attorney William Macmillan, general manager Don Kellett and two other owners, Bruce Livie and Zanvyl Krieger. The other owners joining the 1953 franchise were Bill Hilgenberg and Tom Mullan. Rosenbloom later bought out all his partners.

47

A man with a long and productive affiliation in Baltimore sports, including pro football, baseball and ice hockey, is Zanvyl Krieger, who sparked the battle to have the Colts returned to the NFL in 1953. Krieger is an attorney and owner of the Lord Baltimore Hotel.

It's a man-to-man confrontation as Royce Womble, Colts' running back, attempts to drive through Val Joe Walker of the Green Bay Packers in this 1955 game, a year when the club made its move to become a future title challenger.

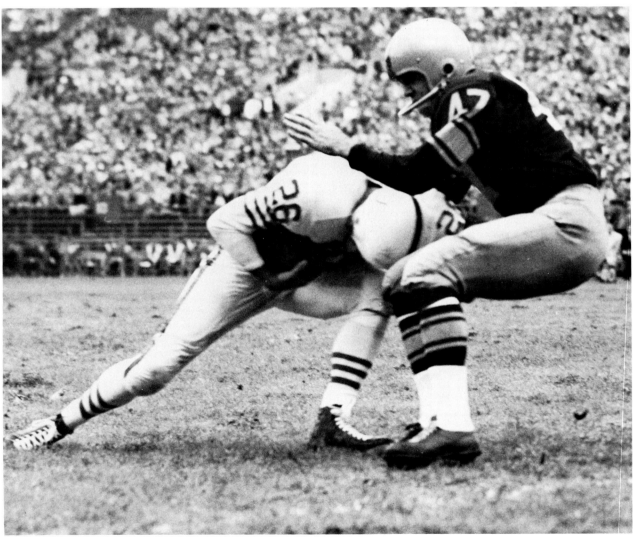

Guard Art Spinney, converted from defensive end, hits the blocking sled. A highly dependable performer and an All-Pro selection.

(Left) Training camp at Westminster, Md., for the Colts was a time for players and coaches to visit with their fans. Here Don Shula, defensive halfback, tries his helmet on Bobby West, age 4, during a break in practice.

Bantam-sized Buddy Young shows his versatility in this 1954 contest with the Chicago Bears. It is generally agreed that Young was one of the most exciting performers in the history of pro football. He later joined the Colts as an official and then moved to the league office under Commissioner Pete Rozelle.

Agile and swift, Milt Davis was another prized pickup. He was signed as a free agent and played a corner for the Colts defense when it won back-to-back titles.

Considered one of the finest blockers the Colts ever had, Jim Mutscheller also was a sure pass receiver in pressure situations. In his first season with the Colts, 1953, Mutscheller played both offense and defense. He was of average physical build but had excellent balance and coordination. Quarterbacks could rely on him when the game was "up for grabs".

A Colt vs. a colt. Author John Steadman, when he was an official of the Colts, staged a foot race before the annual intra-squad game between Dixie, the Colts' mascot, and fleet-footed Buddy Young. That's Allan Zimmerman in the saddle. Young won the 100-yard dash but admittedly beat the starting gun by a few leaps and bounds.

Shifty and nifty in the open field and especially adept at finding the end-zone, L.G. (Long Gone) Dupre was a highly respected halfback for five seasons with the Colts (1955-1959).

He was once described as being as "tough as a piece of steel cable." It's center Madison (Buzz) Nutter, who was signed by the Colts as a free agent after being cut by the Redskins.

A gifted passer and swift afoot, quarterback George Shaw of Oregon was the Colts' bonus choice in 1955. He made the all-rookie team but the next year injured his knee against the Bears and gave way to a player who made an indelible mark in the NFL . . . a then veritable unknown named John Unitas.

When the Baltimore Colts turned loose
Heisman Trophy winner Billy Vessels (No.
21) he was a strong, effective runner. Vessels
started two games for the Colts in 1956 but
gained well over 100 yards each time. He's
shown bringing back a kick against the
Washington Redskins as L.G. (Long Gone)
Dupre (No. 45) and Bill Pellington (No. 36)
lead interference for him.

It was impossible to predict what the future held for
these two young men when this picture was taken
in the Colts' office after they were drafted in 1956.
On the right is Lenny Moore, who made the Hall of
Fame. And the other player? He decided to go to
the Canadian League with the Montreal Alouettes
but later came back to Maryland. That's right,
you're looking at Bob Pascal, chief executive of
Anne Arundel County and mentioned as a possible
future governor. Pascal a Duke product; Moore
from Penn State.

The night before a game was time to relax. Herb Wright, the Colts' business manager, talks with John Unitas and Alan Ameche, in their room. Their expressions reflect a serious mood but maybe all they were wondering about was where they could buy two tickets for an already soldout game.

Durable and determined, Alex Sandusky earned respect among his contemporaries as an outstanding guard. He was from Clarion (Pa.) State Teachers College and came to the Colts as an end but made an easy transition to his pro position, which he handled as a starter for 13 years.

Gene "Big Daddy" Lipscomb shows here why he was one of the most feared and respected defensive tackles in the history of the game (Al Barry, No. 66 of the Green Bay Packers, can attest to that). Adding additional pressure are Artie Donovan, (70) and Don Joyce (83).

Part of the enthusiasm generated for the Colts came from the concept of fan clubs, called Colts' Corrals, which were organized in 1947. The first banner is held by Leo Novak, one of the co-founders, and GM Don Kellett. More than 30 Corrals have been formed, including one in the Maryland State Penitentiary.

Regarded as one of the finest all-around players the Colts ever had, Bert Rechichar at times played safety, offensive end and halfback, returned punts and kickoffs and cared for the field goals, kicking off and extra points. He set a then world record of 56 yards in 1953 in his first pro attempt at a field goal.

The Colts have never had a problem with lack of fan support as evidenced here when 4,000 fans welcomed home the team after defeating the Bears 29-14 in November 1957. That's big Artie Donovan, on the far left, emerging from the plane.

NATIONAL FOOTBALL LEAGUE
STANDARD PLAYERS CONTRACT

BETWEEN

...BALTIMORE. FOOTBALL. INC...... A. CORPORATION. OF. THE. STATE. OF. MARYLAND
which operates **BALTIMORE. COLTS. FOOTBALL. CLUB**., and which is a member of the National Football
League, and which is hereinafter called the "Club," and .... **John. Unitas**................. of
..... **Pittsburgh,. Pennsylvania** ..... hereinafter called the "Player."

In consideration of the respective promises herein the parties hereto agree as follows:

1. The term of this contract shall be from the date of execution hereof until the first day of May following the close of the football season commencing in ...**1956**................, subject however, to rights of prior termination as specified herein.

2. The Player agrees that during the term of this contract he will play football and will engage in activities related to football only for the Club and as directed by the Club according to the Constitution, By-Laws, Rules and Regulations of the National Football League, hereinafter called the "League," and of the Club, and the Club, subject to the provisions hereof, agrees during such period to employ the Player as a skilled football player. The Player agrees during the term of this contract to report promptly for the Club's training seasons to render his full time services during the training seasons and at the Club's direction to participate in all practise sessions and in all League and other football games scheduled by the Club.

3. For the Player's services as a skilled football player during the term of this contract, and for his agreement not to play football or engage in activities related to football for any other person, firm, corporation or institution during the term of this contract, and for the option hereinafter set forth giving the Club the right to renew this contract, and for the other undertakings of the Player herein, the Club promises to pay the Player each football season during the term of this contract the sum of $. **7,000**........ to be payable as follows:

   75% of said salary in weekly installments commencing with the first and ending with the last regularly scheduled League game played by the Club during such season and the balance of 25% of said sum at the end of said last regularly scheduled League game.

In addition, the Club promises and agrees to pay the reasonable board and lodging expenses of the Player incurred while playing games for the Club in other than the Club's home city and also to pay all proper and necessary travelling expenses of the Player and his meals en route to and from said games.

4. The Player agrees at all times to comply with and to be bound by all the provisions of the Constitution, By-Laws, Rules and Regulations of the League and of the Club, all of which are hereby made a part of this contract. If the Player fails to comply with said Constitution, By-Laws, Rules and Regulations the Club shall have the right to terminate this contract or to take such other action as may be specified in said Constitution, By-laws, Rules and Regulations, or as may be directed by the Commissioner of the League, hereinafter called the "Commissioner." The Player agrees to submit himself to the discipline of the League and of the Club for any violation of such Constitution, By-laws, Rules and Regulations subject however, to the right to a hearing by the Commissioner. All matters in dispute between the Player and the Club shall be referred to the Commissioner and his decision shall be accepted as final, complete, conclusive, binding and unappealable, by the Player and by the Club. The Player hereby waives any and all rights of action against the Commissioner, the League, the Club or any of its members or stockholders, and against any officer of the Club or of the League arising out of or in connection with decisions of the Commissioner, except to the extent of awards made by the Commissioner to the Player. The Player hereby acknowledges that he has read said Constitution, By-Laws, Rules and Regulations and that he understands their meaning.

5. The Player promises and agrees that during the term of this contract he will not play football or engage in activities related to football for any other person, firm, corporation or institution except with the prior written consent of the Club and the Commissioner, and that he will not during the term of this contract engage in any game or exhibition of baseball, basketball, hockey, wrestling boxing or any other sport which endangers his ability to perform his services hereunder, without the prior written consent of the Club. The Player likewise promises and agrees that during the term of this contract, when, as and if he shall receive an invitation to participate in any All-Star football game which is approved by the League, he will play in said game in accordance with all the terms and conditions relating thereto, including the player compensation therein set forth, as are agreed to between the League and the Sponsor of such game.

6. The Player represents and warrants that he is and will continue to be sufficiently highly skilled in all types of football team play to play professional football of the caliber required by the League and by the Club, that he is and will continue to be in excellent physical condition, and agrees to perform his services hereunder to the complete satisfaction of the Club and its Head Coach. If in the opinion of the Head Coach the Player does not maintain himself in excellent physical condition or fails at any time during the football seasons included in the term of this contract to demonstrate sufficient skill and capacity to play professional football of the caliber required by the League and by the Club, or if in the opinion of the Head Coach the Player's work or conduct in the performance of this contract is unsatisfactory as compared with the work and conduct of other members of the Club's squad of players, the Club shall have the right to terminate this contract upon written notice to the player of such termination.

7. Upon termination of this contract the Club shall pay the Player only the balance remaining due him for travelling and board and lodging expenses and any balance remaining due him for football seasons completed prior to termination, and, if termination takes place during a football season, any balance remaining due him on that portion of his total compensation for that season as provided in paragraph 3 hereof which the number of regularly scheduled League games already played by the Club during that season bears to the total number of League games scheduled for the Club for that season.

8. The Player hereby represents that he has special, exceptional and unique knowledge, skill and ability as a football player, the loss of which cannot be estimated with any certainty and cannot be fairly or adequately compensated by damages and therefore agrees that the Club shall have the right, in addition to any other rights which the Club may possess, to enjoin him by appropriate injunction proceedings against playing football or engaging in activities related to football for any person, firm, corporation or institution and against any other breach of this contract.

9. It is mutually agreed that the Club shall have the right to sell, exchange, assign and transfer this contract and the Player's services to any other Club of the League and the Player agrees to accept such assignment and to report promptly to the assignee club and faithfully to perform and carry out this contract with the assignee club as if it had been entered into by the Player with the assignee club instead of with this club.

10. On or before the date of expiration of this contract, the Club may, upon notice in writing to the Player, renew this contract for a further term until the first day of May following said expiration on the same terms as are provided by this contract, except that (1) the Club may fix the rate of compensation to be paid by the Club to the Player during said period of renewal, which compensation shall not be less than ninety percent (90%) of the amount paid by the Club to the Player during the preceding season, and (2) after such renewal this contract shall not include a further option to the Club to renew the contract; the phrase "rate of compensation" as above used shall not be understood to include bonus payments or payments of any nature whatsoever other than the precise sum set forth in Paragraph 3 hereof.

11. Player acknowledges the right and power of the Commissioner of the National Football League (a) to fine and suspend, (b) to fine and suspend for life or indefinitely, and/or (c) to cancel the contract of, any player who accepts a bribe or who agrees to throw or fix a game or who, having knowledge of the same, fails to report an offered bribe or an attempt to throw or fix a game, or who bets on a game, or who is guilty of any conduct detrimental to the welfare of the National Football League or of professional football; and the Player hereby releases the Commissioner of the National Football League, individually and in his official capacity, and also the National Football League and every club and every officer, director and stockholder of the League and of every club thereof, jointly, and severally, from all claims and demands for damages and every claim and demand whatsoever he may have arising out of or in connection with the decision of said Commissioner of the National Football League in any of the aforesaid cases.

12. Any payments made hereunder to the Player for a period during which he is entitled to workman's compensation benefits by reason of temporary total, permanent total, temporary partial, or permanent partial disability shall be deemed an advance payment of compensation benefits due the player, and the club shall be entitled to be reimbursed the amounts thereof out of any award of compensation.

13. This agreement contains the entire agreement between the parties and there are no oral or written inducements, promises or agreements except as contained herein.. This agreement shall become valid and binding upon each party hereto only when, as and if it shall be approved by the Commissioner.

14. This agreement has been made under and shall be governed by the laws of the State of **MARYLAND** ....

....

IN WITNESS WHEREOF the Player has hereunto set his hand and seal and the Club has caused this contract to be executed by its duly authorized officer on the date set opposite their respective names.

WITNESS:

Margaret A. Madigan 1/26/56

Mrs. John C. Unitas 1/31/56

BALTIMORE. FOOTBALL. INC.,
Club

D. Kellett
President

John C. Unitas
Player

Approved Bert Bell 2/6/56
Commissioner Date

1509. Creedmore. Avenue...............
Player's Address
Pittsburgh,. Pennsylvania

This Copy to be Sent to Commissioner for Approval
Return to Member Club

*A very hist
document.
contract.*

CHAPTER THREE
GREAT DISCOVERY

When John Constantine Unitas headed for the Baltimore Colts' training camp at Westminster, Md., in July of 1956, he was only hoping for a chance, the professional opportunity that had been denied him the year before when he had been with the Pittsburgh Steelers for the pre-season period and then was sent home jobless.

With the Steelers, he usually played catch on the side of the practice field with the sons of Art Rooney, the club owner. But Walt Kiesling, the head coach, never thought enough of John to even try him for a single play in an exhibition game. So Unitas got a quick shuffle, the same as others before him and, no doubt, some in the future will receive.

He went back to Pittsburgh disappointed but still wanting to play football. He went to work for a drilling company, after coming home from the training base, and on week-ends performed for the Bloomfield Rams, a semi-pro team. He made $6 a game and the right, if he was lucky, to take a cold shower when the game was over instead of having to travel home in his dirty uniform.

The only man we ever knew who saw Unitas in those days was the late Herb Wolfe, who came to Baltimore much later to be director of the Maryland School for the Blind, but, at the time, was employed at the Pennsylvania School for the Blind. "I had a friend who was an official in this semi-pro league around Pittsburgh and he kept telling me about this quarterback who looked so good," recalled Wolfe before he died in 1977.

"He insisted I come out to watch this kid. I didn't want to do it but, at his persuasion, I finally agreed. It was obvious this was a skilled quarterback, much better than any of the players he was with, but, of course, there was no way for anyone to tell he was going to go on to become a standout with the Colts.

"The field he was playing on that night hardly had a blade of grass. I'm not sure it measured 100-yards. And before the game started, they oiled the field to keep the dust down. That was the first time I saw Johnny Unitas."

So it was the Bloomfield Rams who served as Unitas' "finishing school". The Colts signed him for an 80 cent telephone call, after Kellett picked his name off an old waiver list, before or after he got the post-card tip.

The Colts signed Unitas on January 31, 1956. They had him and other free-agents in for a one day practice session later in the spring. The workout was held on a spread of grass along the side of the Clifton Park Swimming Pool. It wasn't a football field, only an open area. Ewbank was impressed with Unitas and so was the team equipment manager, Fred Schubach, who later became a Colts' scout and personnel director. Others weren't sure.

But when the 1956 training period arrived, Unitas was just another name on the Colts roster. He arrived in an old, old used car that was heard well in advance of his pulling into the parking lot at Western Maryland College. The workouts that year found the attention centered on Shaw, a quarterback who could run like a rabbit, had an accurate arm and a 140 IQ.

In Unitas' early days in camp, we were involved in preparing advance publicity for a future exhibition in Louisville, where Unitas had gone to school. We told him what we wanted and asked if he would make a radio spot. "I'll be glad to do it," he answered, "but do you really think I'll be with the club by the time we play in Louisville?" Little did anyone realize what was going to happen.

Events were to prove that it wasn't to be Shaw's year. He was hit by pneumonia in camp, was put in the hospital for treatment and when the Colts went to Boston to play the Giants, the exhibition promoters were unhappy that Unitas was going to have to play in place of the well publicized Shaw. The Giants won, 28-10, and Unitas gave only a mediocre performance, certainly nothing to indicate he was destined for the stature that was to come later.

When Shaw regained his strength, he returned to being the No. 1 QB and that's what he was doing on Oct. 21, 1956 in Wrigley Field, Chicago, against the Bears. Tackle Fred Williams put a strong rush on Shaw, caught him with a clean tackle and tore the ligaments in his knee. The Colts then had to turn to Unitas. It was No. 19 to the center of the stage for better or for worse.

It would be in the best tradition of a Hollywood story-line to say Unitas was an instant success, a star who was born when he, the understudy, took over for the featured performer in an emergency situation. But it wasn't that way at all.

The first pass Unitas attempted, a hitch intended for Mutscheller, was completed but to a player in a differenct colored jersey. It was J.C. Caroline who picked off the near diagonal toss and went streaking for the goal-line, 59-yards away. So Unitas was one-for-one, a touchdown, but it was in behalf of the Bears.

It had been an overwhelming blow to the Colts' morale to have Shaw eliminated so suddenly. The

Unitas is pictured here with Don Shinnick (left) and Raymond Berry in an early training camp photograph taken at Western Maryland College. Check out those ar

Colts' fell apart, fumbling the ball away four times. Unitas wasn't able to move the offense and the final score found the Bears pulling away to win easily, 58-27. But Ewbank insisted all was not lost. He truly believed in Unitas, if others didn't.

From that point on in the season, the Colts played a controlled type of offense. The Colts searched for a quarterback and even brought Gary Kerkorian out of retirement as a backup. They defeated the Green Bay Packers and Cleveland Browns and Unitas gained confidence and the team in him. Against the Rams in Baltimore, he "arrived". The Colts won, 56-21, and at one point in the game Bert Rose, the Rams' public relations director, later to be general manager of the Minnesota Vikings and New Orleans Saints, jumped up from his seat in the press box and exclaimed, "I don't believe it. I just saw that kid throw a pass 30 yards into a six-inch opening."

It later turned out, through a check of the Rams' files, that they had 21 pages of scouting reports on Unitas when he was a college player. The Colts, conversley, had only his name but they wound up with Unitas because of Kellett's alert follow-up phone call.

There was growing enthusiasm building for Unitas and much respect, too, on behalf of his teammates. A reporter in Los Angeles, as the Colts were winding down the season, wrote that "Shaw was now playing second fiddle". So every time we would see Shaw, in the hotel lobby or the training room he would strike the pose of a fiddle player using his arm as a simulated bow.

Unitas was being talked about as a prize discovery, which he was. George Preston Marshall, owner of the Washington Redskins, even put out an erroneous story that Unitas came to the Colts because the line coach, Herman Ball, had been in Pittsburgh the year before, under head coach Kiesling, and knew Unitas was a youngster of talent. But that was a mistake. Ball didn't remember much about Unitas, admitted it and never tried to take credit for John coming to Baltimore.

Even a road roller couldn't get to John Unitas when he was preparing to pass, as evidenced by this picture taken in training camp. Line coach Herman Ball is on the heavy duty machine as Alex Sandusky, Madison (Buzz) Nutter and Art Spinney (l. to r.) set-up to playfully block the "mechanical monster".

The fact that the Steelers missed Unitas was to become a total embarrassment for them. Kiesling went to his grave still not convinced Unitas was as good as the record book and his consistent performances showed. But the rest of the Steelers' organization, Rooney and his boys, all knew a superb talent had been let to slip away.

In an early exhibition the next year, 1957, the Colts bombed out the Steelers in Cincinnati. The following day, a Sunday, Unitas stopped in Pittsburgh before coming back to camp at Westminster and was driving down a main street. He pulled up to a red light and in an adjoining lane, coincidentally, was a car with Rooney driving, Kiesling in the passenger seat and some young Rooneys in the back. Unitas leaned over and hollered, "Hello, Mr. Rooney," The signal quickly changed and traffic moved on.

Running the bootleg play was sometimes a surprise move for John Unitas. No. 19 is sprinting to the outside against the Green Bay Packers in 1957 while Alan (The Horse) Ameche (No. 35), Art Spinney (No. 63) and Alex Sandusky (No. 68) show the way.

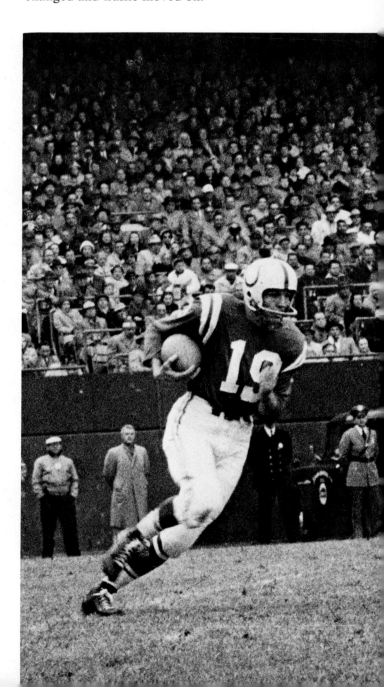

Rooney's sons were to say, "Dad, that was Johnny Unitas". It was the first time Rooney had ever seen him close up. A few blocks down the street, they were stopped by another light. Rooney looked over and said, "John, I wish you a lot of success and hope you become the greatest quarterback the league has ever had". Unitas thanked him and again they drove away, as the light went from red to green.

Rooney, in relating the story later, said he felt ashamed he had mentioned those things to Unitas in front of Kiesling because he figured it was throwing salt in a fresh and painful wound. Kiesling, on that occasion, never uttered a word and finally the cars separated in traffic and went their separate ways.

The manner in which Unitas started to perform meant that Shaw never got his job back, similar to what happened in baseball when Lou Gehrig took over first base with the New York Yankees from injured Wally Pipp and went on to play 2,130 consecutive games.

Unitas got his first attention nationally when *The Sporting News,* in its "Quarterback" supplement. carried a full page on Unitas, the little known quarterback of the Colts. Author Jimmy Breslin followed up with a piece in *The Saturday Evening Post* and now the country was getting excited about the Cinderella kid from the other side of the tracks, who had played at tiny St. Justin High School in Pittsburgh and wanted to go to Notre Dame and Indiana but was turned down in both places and finally wound up at Louisville.

His mother, widowed when John was a child, had to take a job with the City of Pittsburgh cleaning office buildings at night to keep food on the table

and clothes on the backs of the family. On two occasions, John was involved in shooting accidents that could have impaired his chances of ever becoming a football player.

Once he was coming home from school and neighborhood youths were playing on a lot with a live cartridge. They hit the bottom of it and the discharging bullet pierced John's leg. Another time, he was playing with a gun they had in the house, for protection against prowlers, and it discharged, damaging his hand. Both injuries were fortunately superficial but could have been tragic.

The 1956 season saw Unitas collaborate with Mutscheller, one of his most dependable receivers, to save the job of Ewbank, who was on the ropes and about to be fired. Rosenbloom was unhappy and didn't feel the coaching was what it should be. It was believed Rosenbloom was considering Buddy Parker or Joe Kuharich to be the new head coach, but it never happened.

What was supposed to be Ewbank's demise came out differently. The Colts trailed the Washington Redskins in the final minutes when Unitas fired far down field. The pass was about to be intercepted by Norb Hecker of the Redskins but the ball bounced off his shoulder pads into the arms of Mutscheller, who put on a determined effort to claw his way into the end-zone. It was a spectacular 19-17 ending to a game it appeared the Colts were going to lose. So Rosenbloom decided to stay with Ewbank, mostly because the fans were in a happy state of mind. It was a wise decision because of what was to happen later.

Unitas had a strong arm, a quick mind and was absolutely beyond intimidation. When a game was lost, he didn't come into the locker room and go into a shell or break up the furnishings. He merely accepted the fact he had prepared himself and given his best, and he realized no amount of screaming or complaining was about to change the result. He was, most of the time, no different following victory or defeat.

He became a master of the check-off, changing signals at the line of scrimmage when the defense was stacked against the play he called in the huddle. "He's some man," praised guard Art Spinney. "He knows how to play and will hang-in there when times are tough. No question about it, he's our 'meal ticket'. You have to respect that man. I have the feeling he's going to take us a long way."

Bob Waterfield, one of the premier quarterbacks in all of football, saw Unitas in those early days and said his greatest skill was in "looking off receivers", meaning John could direct his attention to one area, fake the pass there and come back to an entirely different part of the field and hit another receiver who was coming open. With a game up for grabs and the clock moving, Unitas could extract the maximum, sometimes 12 to 15 plays in a two minute span.

With all the attention that came to him, there wasn't any spoiled attitude apparent. He was "one of the boys" frequently travelling with Bert Rechichar, Andy Nelson and Alex Sandusky and not doing much more than drinking beer and eating hamburgers when he stopped off in a neighborhood bar. After the 1957 season, he was the recipient of the Jim Thorpe Memorial Award, given out by the NEA, as the league's most valuable player. The presentation was to be made in New York.

"Go with Unitas and make sure he finds his way," said Kellett, so the two of us got on the train and went to a New York television studio. We asked Unitas during the trip if he had ever been to New York before. He said yes, when the University of Louisville had earlier played in a post-season basketball tournament at Madison Square Garden.

He slept on the floor of a friend's room in a hotel because he only had 35 cents in his pocket. Unitas was unspoiled, didn't believe the world owed him a living and found football a distinct pleasure, plus the fact he was being paid for it. It never upset him what other players were making, like when Joe Namath signed a record $400,000 contract with the New York Jets.

Asked his reaction to Namath getting such a high salary, he merely said, "My mother always told me to be happy if you have one loaf of bread under your arm; you don't need two." And that was the way he dismissed the financial fact that Namath was being paid much more than he was and hadn't accomplished what he did.

Unitas was to represent much to America, not only as a football player but as a personality...the kid who wasn't born with a silver spoon in his mouth, who knew adversity all his life and made it to the summit of success on courage and fortitude. His ability could never be denied or diminished.

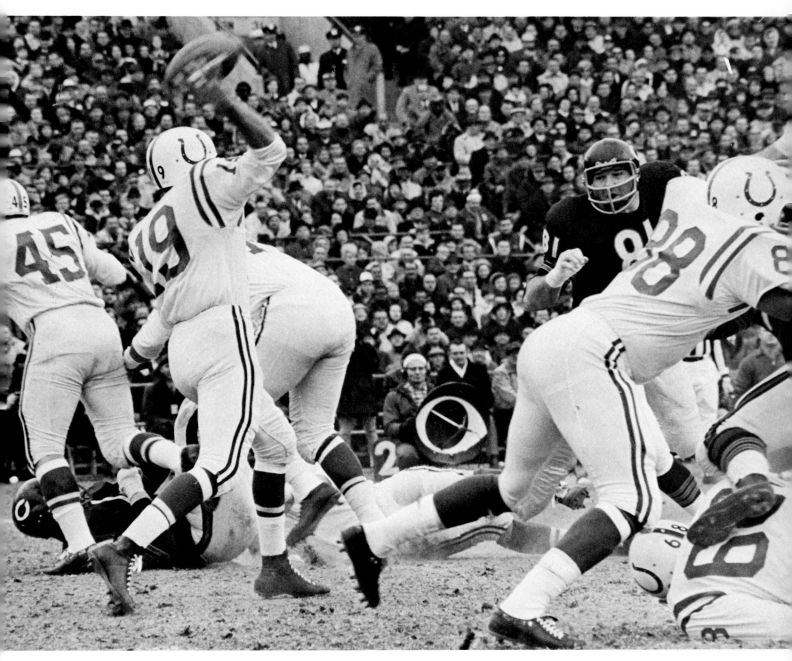

Colt fans will remember this passing motion for years and years to come. Providing the protection for Unitas are Jerry Hill (45) and John Mackey (88) as Bear defender Doug Atkins struggles to break through.

COLTS WIN FIRST "SUDDEN DEA...

...orld's title.

FIRST SUDDEN DEATH GAME
OFFICIAL
COLTS 23-17 GIANTS

BALTIMORE
COLTS
1958-59
"WORLD CHAMPIONS"

CHAPTER FOUR
TWO WORLD TITLES

What happened to the Baltimore Colts on Dec. 28, 1958 and the city and state it represented has never been equalled or surpassed. There was mass hysteria resulting from the outcome of a single but, yes, exceptional football game. The Colts had done for Baltimore what no team since the grand Old Orioles of the National League accomplished when they won the Temple Cup, forerunner to the World Series, in 1894, 1895 and 1896.

But there were far more witnesses, 64,185, to what the Colts attained in Yankee Stadium against the New York Giants. There also was a major television network that carried the game coast-to-coast to an estimated 45 million viewers and a radio hookup around the globe. What followed in the way of unrestrained enthusiasm was somewhat akin to what took place after World War I and World War II, when the great conflicts were over. But this was a sporting event and that made it different. There was reason for pure joy with no casualty counts to tear at hearts and dampen the eyes.

The Colts had an impressive campaign in 1958 as they built to the title showdown. But midway in the schedule, Unitas was "raked" by John Symank of the Green Bay Packers and suffered a punctured lung. He couldn't play. The Colts had to turn to George Shaw, who hadn't started a game in two years, back to the day he was hurt, and hoped he could make a contribution. In fact, he went against the Giants and Bears, the team that had temporarily curtailed his career on the same field two years before.

Against the Giants, a foe the Colts were to later face for the title, six weeks away, they lost a close 24-21 contest. Shaw quarterbacked and was disconsolate after the loss. "I feel like this was my chance to help the team with Unitas out. I'm unhappy and upset we didn't win," he commented as he sat all alone with his thoughts on the train trip home from New York after the game. But there was no reason for Shaw to fault himself. He wasn't the reason the Colts didn't win. In fact, he had an early touchdown pass dropped in the end-zone and had thrown for all three of the Colts' scores. Unitas, watching on television in Union Memorial Hospital, thought Shaw had been superb and shouldn't berate himself.

This photograph, taken at the Pro Football Hall of Fame, displays a few of the momento's from the 1958 Sudden Death victory over the New York Giants.

"When the Giants' game was over, Charley Conerly, lending his name to a ghost-column in the *New York Journal American,* made the mistake of allowing himself to write "we out-gutted them". The comment irked the Colts and they seized on it as their battle cry as they later prepared to play the Giants for the championship.

But before that came about, the Colts had to earn the Western Division championship. They beat the San Francisco 49ers in what most of the players and this observer agree, along with veteran announcers Chuck Thompson and Vince Bagli, was the "greatest game ever played"...not the sudden death victory. The players believe if they wouldn't have whipped the 49ers they wouldn't have had a championship to play in Yankee Stadium.

They trailed the 49ers, 27-7, at halftime but came back to score 28 points during the last two periods. A remarkable run by Moore that was considered by many of his admirers as the best he ever made tied the score at 27-27 and Steve Myhra added the point that finally sent the Colts ahead. It started as a simple end run, with Berry and Spinney clearing the way, but Moore zig and zagged, feinted, cut back, utilized the sidelines and then picked up Preas as his final escort across the faraway goal line. "Something just told me to 'run, Lenny, run', and that's all I was trying to do," explained Moore later. It comes close to being the greatest individual running effort in the history of the franchise.

Meanwhile, the Colts defense was doing a job on the 49ers, completely shutting down an offense that had such talented performers as Tittle, Hugh McElhenny, Joe Perry, Billy Wilson and Gordon Soltau. The win meant the Colts clinched the division because news came over the Western Union wire that the Pittsburgh Steelers knocked off the Bears, who were the Colts' closest pursuers. That night, as the Colts celebrated at Art Donovan's Valley Country Club, the late Ray Krouse, a strong tackle-end, who was a friend of Bobby Layne's, the Steeler QB, decided they should show their appreciation for the fact he had quarterbacked the win over the Bears.

So a group of six Colts made a contribution to buy Layne a gift. It was most appropriate. They bought and sent him a set of long-stemmed toasting glasses. The question still to be decided had to do with whether the Colts would be playing the Giants or Browns. A Cleveland-Baltimore match-up, pitting Ewbank against Brown, would have been a natural but it didn't work out that way. The Giants whipped the Browns, 10-0 in a playoff, and qualified to meet the Colts.

In 1958, after John Unitas was injured in mid-season, the Colts brought Gary Kerkorian out of retirement for quarterback insurance. Around the blackboard with Coach Weeb Ewbank are Kerkorian, George Shaw and Ray Brown. Kerkorian and Brown later became attorneys and Shaw a stock broker after their pro football days.

He wasn't celebrated for his running but John Unitas is shown jogging around Memorial Stadium, football in hand, while recovering from broken ribs and a punctured lung in 1958. He missed two games but returned to lead the Colts to a showdown with the New York Giants for the 1958 NFL title.

It has never been spelled-out how it happened but the Colts had a chance to "spy" on the Giants that week leading up to the championship. The information wasn't all that important but it gave the Colts the comforting knowledge that the Giants, except for a double reverse involving Frank Gifford, weren't planning to do anything differently against them. They were well prepared and approached the game with confidence. An estimated 12,000 Baltimore fans went to New York for the battle.

The Colts took the field primed for an all-out effort. They went to New York determined to make Conerly regret what he had earlier permitted his literary "ghost" to say in the newspaper. They also received a motivating talk from Ewbank in the locker room. He spoke with personal references to most of the players, citing how Buzz Nutter had been picked from the waiver list after being cut by the Washington Redskins and how Bill Pellington had been released by the Cleveland Browns and how he had let Donovan go from the Browns, keeping, instead, John Sandusky, because he was a two-way tackle.

By actual count, 14 of the 35 Colts had been found wanting by other teams. So now Ewbank told them this was the time to prove to the world at large they had ability and could handle the Giants. It was, for the most part, an experienced team since only three rookies, Ray Brown, John Sample and Lenny Lyles, made the 1958 squad. And in the title game, it was Brown, besides playng a safety position, who punted for a near championship average record of 51 yards.

Marchetti served notice to the Giants on the first play he was going to be difficult to handle. He quickly put a rush on Conerly and interrupted the Giants' offensive timing. Before they could get anything started, Marchetti was there to be a source of physical annoyance.

The Giants had to settle for a Pat Summerall field goal from the 36-yard line in the first period after it appeared Alex Webster was about to make a catch for a certain first down or even a touchdown at the 15. But Webster lost his footing and, even though the ball was thrown perfectly, he wasn't in position to catch it.

The Colts got an early invitation to score after Gene (Big Daddy) Lipscomb and Ray Krouse, both deceased, crashed into Gifford and caused him to fumble. Moore and Alan (The Horse) Ameche quickly took the ball to the two, where Ameche went in for the tally behind Spinney and Parker. That made the score 7-3.

There was an exchange of fumbles that could have turned the game around right there. Jackie Simpson bobbled a punt at the 11 and the Giants recovered but then Gifford was blasted with another jarring

Running down ball carriers was another specialty of Gino Marchetti, who also made life miserable for quarterbacks. Marchetti was 6-foot-4, 242 pounds and came off the mark with the quickness of a halfback. He was one of the few players in Colts' history who actually enjoyed the heavy duty program of training camp, even if the thermometer read 98 degrees in the shade. He's shown here stopping Ram halfback Jon Arnett during the 1958 championship season.

tackle and Don Joyce got the ball back for Baltimore. So the Colts were extracted from another tight spot.

Most of the second period was consumed with a Colts' drive of 86 yards in 15 plays, Unitas passing to Berry for the final 15 yards and a TD that made the score 14-3 at halftime. Ewbank told the club during intermission to assume it was two touchdowns behind and needed two more to win in the second half.

The 1958 season meant much to laughing boys Art Donovan and Gino Marchetti. It was their first time on a championship club and they obviously loved every minute of it.

Following what is regarded as one of the Colts' greatest victories, a come-from-behind win over the San Francisco 49ers, three game standouts group together in the locker room with Coach Weeb Ewbank. Left to right are Raymond Berry, who scored in the last minutes to assure the triumph; Lenny Moore, who made a spectacular 73 yard TD run, and John Unitas, who scored once and passed for another six-pointer. The win clinched the Western Division title in 1958.

Another extensive push, this one for 58-yards, took the Colts to a first down at the Giants' one-yard line. If the Colts score here then the margin goes to 20-3 or 21-3 and then the Giants would have to live dangerously and throw caution to the wind. The game might have broken wide-open and there would have been no sudden-death aspect to set it apart.

But the Giants turned them back with a determined stand, stopping Ameche three times and Unitas once. The last play, just a yard away from a score, found Ameche turning outside on an option pass. He could keep it himself or toss to Mutscheller. But he never had a chance. Cliff Livingston read what was coming and came through to cut off Ameche, the Colts losing four yards on the final down.

This gave the Giants a quick lift. It didn't take long for them to come back. It was a bizarre play that took them from their own 13 to the Colts' one. Kyle Rote made a stretching catch of a Conerly pass at the 45 and ran 20 more yards as Milt Davis and Carl Taseff missed tackles. Andy Nelson hauled down Rote, who fumbled, but Webster was along side of him to pick it up and then he started running, like a relay race. He almost made it, only a yard short of the goal, when Taseff, who got off the ground, started running too, and brought Webster down barely short of the final stripe. But this served only as a delaying action. Mel Triplett banged across at 11:14 of the third period and now the Colts' lead was reduced to 14-10. The Giants were far from giving up.

Conerly reached Bob Schnelker with two picture passes and then pitched to Gifford for the touchdown that put the Giants in control at 17-14 at the top of the fourth quarter. Another climactic moment arrived much later in the period on third and four at the Giants' 25. If the Giants made it they could have controlled the ball for another series. Gifford hit the right side and got almost all that was needed, except for a foot. Lipscomb and Marchetti were under the pile of defenders. But Gino couldn't get up. His foot was bent. It took six stretcher-bearers to get him off the field with what was later announced as a fractured ankle.

Referee Ron Gibbs, meanwhile had taken a chain measurement and said the Giants had come up short. The Giants decided to stay with the percentages and punt the ball away, Don Chandler kicking to Taseff on a fair catch at the 14. There were less than two minutes to play, the Colts were behind three points and positioned 86-yards from the goal-line. Two passes failed and then Unitas crossed-up the Giants by handing off to Moore, who got 11-quick yards and a first down. A typical Unitas call. A shocker.

The Colts were fighting the Giants and also the

End Jim Mutscheller and head coach Weeb Ewbank are shown here conferring during a workout on Christmas Eve, 1958, just a few days before their showdown with the New York Giants.

clock. Three times Unitas and Berry hooked-up and on each occasion Berry battled for yardage after catching the ball. The third reception connected with Berry at the 25 and he fought to the 13. Only nine seconds remained in the regulation game.

Ewbank hollered for the field goal unit, led by kicker Myhra and holder Shaw. Nutter snapped, Shaw put the ball down at the 19 and Myhra kicked it through the posts to make it 17-17. "I thought to myself if I didn't make it good it was going to be an awfully lonesome winter for me in the wheat fields of the Dakotas," said Myhra later.

So now football was set-up for its first-ever overtime game. Marchetti was being carried off along the sidelines but asked to be put down on the ground so he could sit up and watch temporarily before being taken to the dressing room. The Colts' partisans boomed out a greeting, "Yeah Gino! Yea Gino! Yea Gino!" He waved back.

The flip of the coin for the extra-point found Unitas representing the Colts; Rote and Bill Svoboda the Giants. Referee Gibbs made the toss, Unitas called "tails" but it came down "heads". The Colts would kickoff and the Giants would get first chance to score and end it all.

There was a wave of mounting tension sweeping Yankee Stadium, which had so many times in its storied past been the scene of great drama but nothing like this because it was the first time anything like this had happened. The Giants, after the kickoff, started at their own 20. Gifford tried right end but Joyce and Ordell Braase, who had gone in for Marchetti, brought him down after a four yard advance. Then Conerly tried to reach Schnelker for a first down but the pass missed.

On third down, Conerly intended to pass again but, after fading back, found all receivers covered. He could only run for it and did but, like happened earlier to the Giants, he came up painfully short. They lacked a foot again and once more Chandler punted it away to Taseff.

The Colts took over but were 79 yards from the goal line. As it turned out, they were able to maintain control for 13 consecutive plays as Unitas utilized Dupre and Ameche on the ground and Berry in the air. The Giants were wary of Unitas going to Moore for the game-ender but he kept picking away in other areas.

One time, Unitas, after being jolted by Dick Modzelewski for an eight yard loss, invited him to come again, only John wasn't going to have the ball. They trapped Modzelewski, as Spinney exploded into him from the side. Preas cut-off Sam Huff and Ameche went 24 yards, a chance to go all the way, but he was pulled down at the 20. After Dupre was stopped, Unitas put the ball up again . . .and once more it was to Berry on a slant. He moved all the way to the eight yard line.

Ameche got two yards. Here again, Unitas crossed up the Giants when he daringly threw a flat pass to Mutscheller, who almost made it across the goal line at the one. Later he was to remark that there's "never a risk if you know what you're doing". And high-wire walkers say the same thing.

It remained for Ameche, on the 13th play of overtime, at 8:15, to take it over the right side for the score through an immense hole made possible by Mutscheller blocking Livingston, Preas taking Jim Katcavage and Moore cutting down Emlen Tunnell. The fans spilled onto the field and wrenched the ball away from Ameche as he hit the end-zone but Nutter pulled it back and later the team presented it to Marchetti. It was Spinney who wanted to know, "Who out-gutted who?" and Nutter added, "I guess their hearts weren't as big as their mouths."

Yes, the Colts had won the championship and played an important part in shaping one of pro football's most epic games. *Sports Illustrated* magazine referred to it as "the best game ever played." If not that, then certainly one of the most unforgettable because of its historic impact.

N.Y. GIANTS VS. BALTIM

E COLTS

When the pulsating afternoon was over, this reporter, an old friend of Commissioner Bell, encountered him in the departing mob at Yankee Stadium. He said, "John, ole boy," which was his way of opening almost any conversation, "I never thought I would live to see 'sudden death'." It was a comment that has lived with us until this moment.

Bell, who was overcome with emotion, realized the Colts winning the title proved like never before the importance of the draft. The Colts' victory demonstrated a "down" team could quickly find the path to respectability and a championship. The game also was to have a lasting influence on pro football. Some ugly rumors surfaced that the gamblers had played a part in the outcome. But this was without foundation, pure fiction. The irresponsible talk was based on the fact Unitas passed to Mutscheller near the sidelines in overtime. But the play was there and Unitas, self-assured, said the risk was no different than a simple handoff. Certainly, a team driving for a score could not have been attempting a field goal on any down but the fourth. To do other wise would have been folly. As it was, Ameche stormed over for the historic TD, making it 23-17, on the third down from the one yard line.

With the grace and speed of a gazelle, Lenny Moore is shown here as he turns around end against the New York Giants for a long gainer in the championship showdown of 1958. Alan Ameche is the other Colt in the play. The pursuing Giants are Jim Katcavage (No. 75) and Dick Modzelewski (No. 77).

Look to the left and you can see the focal point of all that goal line activity. The player with his arms clasping the football is Alan Ameche, who is shown as he scored for the first time in the Colts' 1958 title encounter with the Giants.

One of Unitas' many passes is captured here in this classic photograph of the 1958 championship game.

The Colts had no idea what awaited them on the return to Friendship Airport. It was estimated by police that 30,000 well-wishers were on hand to receive them. They spilled all over the runways, which was the first time the airport realized it was going to need to establish a crowd control plan. The mob bordered on hysteria. Some men, women and children were knocked down and all but trampled in the all-out scramble to get close to the Colts.

The players were placed in two buses, after they got off the plane, but some boys and men climbed on the sides of the vehicles and even made it to the roof. A police cruiser had its top crushed the way you would step on a tin-can. Finally, it was determined the only way the Colts might be able to leave the airport was by a back-road escape route. So they went in the opposite direction of Baltimore, turned around near a church and school, with some kids still clinging to the bus, and then headed for the Baltimore-Washington Parkway, letting players off at the Lord Baltimore Hotel and then at Memorial Stadium.

The Baltimore News American came out with a spectacular edition on Monday that sold more copies than any issue since the end of World War II, or until the death of entertainer Elvis Presley in 1977. Even the weather box was tied-in with the Colts. It read "Not So Colt".

The Colts became the talk of the land and the next year, after polishing off the College All-Stars, 29-0, went out and won another NFL crown, and it was all uphill, defying the odds, because they lost three of their first seven games.

But, for some un-explained reason, the Colts continually put themselves in a position of having to do things the hard way. They were forced to win their two final games on the West Coast to win the division, beating the 49ers, 34-14, in Kezar Stadium as the defense intercepted six passes and Unitas threw twice to Berry and once to Moore for scores; and then rolling from behind to jolt the Rams, 45-26.

Heading into the final period, the Rams led, 26-24, but the Colts exploded with three scores in 4 minutes and 40 seconds. Unitas passed to Jerry Richardson for nine yards and Szymanski followed with an interception and a 15-yard touchdown run. Then, to cap the explosive comeback, Taseff picked up a missed field goal and returned it 99-yards for a touchdown.

The outcome set-up another Giants-Colts meeting for the 1959 championship, this one played in Baltimore. It was a freak day, weatherwise, on Dec. 27, as warm, unseasonable temperatures settled over Baltimore. The opposing "pitchers" of the year before, Unitas and Conerly, were matched again. The outcome also was the same, a Baltimore win,

but it didn't take overtime to do it. The Colts won 31-16, as Sample intercepted two Conerly passes late in the game. One of his "steals" went for a 42-yard TD return and a 28-9 bulge and then, with less than three minutes to play, he grabbed another that made it possible for a Myhra field goal.

The Giants didn't score a touchdown all afternoon, or until only 32 seconds were left, Conerly passing to Schnelker. Their other nine points had come from Summerall field goals in each of the first three periods. Unitas completed, in all, 18 or 29 passes for 264 yards but Sample was one of the outstanding defensive players. Szymanski and Lipscomb also sparked the Colts defensive unit and Nutter dominated Huff, the well-publicized middle linebacker, so thoroughly he hardly got a call.

Now, the Colts had earned two NFL championships in succession. It wasn't like the charm of the first time but it never is. If they could win twice, why not go for three? They did, too, but got themselves involved in a brutal physical skirmish with the Bears, a game that Marchetti, Donovan, Unitas, Spinney and the other veterans to this day agree was the hardest hitting game they ever endured.

Unitas passed to Moore for 39-yards and the payoff with only 19 seconds on the clock in a dramatic ending. The battle took so much out of the Colts and Bears neither team was able to win another game the remainder of the season.

So the three-in-a-row dream came to an end but this didn't mean the Colts were through as a title contender. There would be other memorable moments unfolding, games to revel in, and, yes, ones to regret, too.

Gino, broken ankle draped with a towel, looks on anxiously as the Colts were driving downfield for what proved to be one of the most dramatic moments in the history of pro football (below).

Steve Myhra kicks the tying field goal with only nine seconds left to deadlock the New York Giants, 17-17, and send the game into overtime. George Shaw (No. 14) was the holder.

A score in-the-making, one of the most important in the history of the Colts, as Alan (The Horse) Ameche, finds inviting daylight in the sudden death period to give his team its first NFL crown. Ameche got exceptional blocking on the game-winning plunge, as evidenced by the hole his teammates created. An unforgettable celebration followed.

The Weather
Rain ending by afternoon today. High near 50. Yesterday's temperature: High, 55; low, 34.
(Details, Page 23; Map, Page 23.)

THE ☀ SUN FINAL

Vol. 244—No. 36—F   416,219 | Sunday 321,256   BALTIMORE, MONDAY, DECEMBER 29, 1958   26 Pages   5 Cents

COLTS WIN CHAMPIONSHIP

DE GAULLE ANNOUNCES AUSTERITY BUDGET TO REDUCE FRENCH PERIL

Says Nation Is In Dangerous Straits, Must Tighten Financial Belt To Survive; Cuts Include Veterans Pensions

Paris, Dec. 28 (AP)—Premier Charles de Gaulle told the French people tonight the nation was in a dangerous strait and must accept sweeping financial reforms and belt tightening.

Explaining a sharp devaluation of the franc, partial convertibility of the franc in international trade and announcing the freeing of quota restrictions from 90 per cent of France's imports, De Gaulle addressed a nation-wide radio and television audience.

He outlined an austerity budget in cutting into everything from rail fares to politically touchy veterans pensions.

Pinay Supports Pledge

However, de Gaulle promised funds to raise the lowest minimum wage levels as well as unemployment benefits to give bottom-rung workers a guaranteed, if low, annual wage.

Antoine Pinay, de Gaulle's conservative, bespectacled finance Minister, followed him on the nationwide hookup and backed up the de Gaulle promise by saying:

"I solemnly assure you that the standard of living for the lowest paid will not be reduced and that legislation protecting them will be applied with dignity and exactitude."

Pinay also reminded his listeners that the low tax rate, which was devalued 17.55 per cent yesterday to 493.7 to the dollar.

No Algeria Program

The messages for de Gaulle and Pinay were heard through France and its dwindling empire by millions who had been braced for the bad news by black head lines telling of the nation's financial troubles.

It was one of the longest and meatiest addresses the 68-year old Premier has made since returning to power seven months ago. He held out no immediate promise of a better life to the French.

He gave no solution or ending to the nationalist rebellion in Algeria which is the cause of much of France's financial trouble. On the contrary, the cost would likely increase, de Gaulle said. "We have undertaken to improve conditions, particularly for conserving their living standards," de Gaulle said in his sole reference to the troubled territory.

"Very Sacred Catastrophe"

The tall, erect leader of the French in World War II told citizens of the Fifth Republic "I accept the mandate which you confided in me "by electing me president, the office he assumes January 8.

"The national task which fell upon us eighteen years ago this finds itself by this fact, confirmed," he added.

He recalled that when he returned to power seven months ago, with Algeria's settlers and the Army up in arms against the weak Paris Government, France was "on the way toward catastrophe."

"The movement of the month of May, while it first appeared in Algeria, proceeded in reality from the general conviction that the public powers were important against the wave of menaces which comprised, naturally from striking our economy."

"The confidence of the country has permitted us, in this realm, as in others, to reverse the tendency and ward off the catastrophe."

(Continued, Page 4, Column 1)

MONEY MOVES STIR EUROPE

Uncertainty About Long-Term Effect Voiced

London, Dec. 28 (AP) — Western Europe's leap toward freer finance triggered political arguments today—and some uncertainty about the long term effect on people's pocketbooks.

By the time banks open their doors tomorrow morning the francs' convertibility on the continent's main trading markets, in the hope of encouraging wider trade, will have related the regulations for converting their money into foreign currencies.

At the same time, France is pushing for a bigger share of international markets by devaluing the franc and making its goods cheaper for foreign buyers.

Business leaders generally welcomed the decisions announced Saturday, although some were reluctant to forecast the consequences.

Socialist newspapers and left wing leaders like Britain's Hugh Gaitskell called the currency reforms serious mistakes and forecast possible depression and increasing unemployment.

Austrian Move Expected

Under the changes, most of the West European governments guarantee to exchange foreign holdings of their currencies into dollars or any other form of cash.

The limited convertibility was announced by Britain, West Germany, Holland, Belgium, Luxembourg, Denmark, Sweden, Norway, Italy and France.

Newspapers in Vienna predicted that the Austrian Government shortly would announce free convertibility of its schilling.

Businessmen interests in the countries that already have taken the step acknowledged it will mean smart and tighter competition, but were optimistic about their ability to meet it.

The West Berlin Sunday paper Der Tag commented:

"Convertibility has been in preparation for a long time. Its importance exists in the fact that from now on the participating countries will be forced to coordinate their policies."

(Continued, Page 4, Column 2)

Showdown Believed Near As Cuban Rebels Advance

Havana, Dec. 28 (AP)—Cuban Government forces and insurgents were engaged in violent offensives in central and eastern Cuba today.

The pay-off day of the two-year-old civil war appeared close at hand.

Four of Fidel Castro's rebel columns were reported marching on Santiago de Cuba in the east after smashing blows at the Army in Oriente Province.

The rebel radio triumphantly broadcast this report and said the purpose was to set up a separate government in the eastern province soon.

But in central Cuba, President Fulgencio Batista's Government forces aggressively have opened a ferocious offensive to stem a tide of rebel advances which seriously threatened Santa Clara, the capital of Las Villas Province.

While the rebels in Oriente claimed they had begun their

Planes, Artillery Sent

The Government offensive apparently was in the area of Cuba's main central highway east of Santa Clara, possibly in the area of Ranchuelo, one of the points the rebels claimed to have taken.

Reports from Las Villas pictured the Army as delivering smashing blows at rebel positions, army planes and artillery heavily bombed and shelled rebel concentrations in the area surrounding Santa Clara.

The rebels have attempted to declare these places open cities, in order to set up a Government counterattack.

Government forces also were on the move in the eastern areas of Las Villas. A rebel radio broadcast from Jatibonico in Camaguey province near the Las Villas border, said the insurgent-held town was heavily bombed by four Army planes.

The Army had warned civilian populations in towns held or threatened by rebel forces there

THE RUN THAT WON THE GAME — Alan Ameche, Baltimore Colt fullback, has plenty of running room as he booms over for the winning touchdown that beat the New York Giants, 23 to 17, in "sudden death" overtime due the National Football League championship. Lenny Moore (24), at left on the ground, is effectively blocking Emlen Tunnell (45), while Johnny Unitas (19), in rear, watches the action as does Giant Sam Patton (20) in Yankee Stadium.

NEWSPAPER STRIKE ENDS

N.Y. Delivery Union Votes Heavily For Settling

New York, Dec. 28 (AP) — Newspaper deliverers today voted overwhelmingly—2,091 to 537—to end New York's costliest newspaper strike. Morning papers started their presses rolling almost immediately.

The nineteen-day strike was the longest in the city's history involving all nine major New York newspapers.

A loud cheer went up from a crowd of about 1,500 union members and newspaper-started spectators as the result of the vote was announced at the Manhattan Center.

"We are now ready to go back to work with the best wages and working conditions ever had by the members of our union," said Sam Feldman, president of the Mail and Newspaper Deliverers Union. The union's membership had twice turned down negotiated agreements before today's vote.

Happy At End

Asked if he thought the strike had been worthwhile, Feldman said only that he was happy to see it over. A spokesman for the Publishers Association of New York, which represented the newspaper management, said: "The drivers tonight accepted what they twice earlier rejected after prolonged negotiation and despite the advice of their officials."

Multi-night death smashing toll.

The estimated that the strike cost the publishing business almost $25,000,000 in revenue. Other millions were lost outside the newspaper business.

The effect of the strike has been felt in industry trade, cultural life, and almost every element of the city.

(Continued, Page 7, Column 2)

New York Shudders As Colt Fans Romp

By ERNEST B. FURGURSON
[Sun Staff Correspondent]

New York, Dec. 28 — Within seven seconds after Alan Ameche crossed the goal line and the Colts became Pro football's world champions, a Baltimore fan in a blue knit hat was swinging from the crossbar of the goal post.

Banking on the fact everyone was a "bench"ill about 15,000 Colt rooters, who made Yankee Stadium, the north-south subway lines and Pennsylvania Station shudder to a chant that went like this:

Gimme a C!! "C"
Gimme an O!! "O"

And so on—but the difference today was that when C-O-L-T-S. left on the ground, it was all spelled out, the fans' response to "What does that spell?"

"CHAMPS!"

The mass of Baltimore backers swarming out of their biggest stronghold along the erstwhile night-field bleachers to yell for Ameche.

Then one of them played ring-around the rosy.

Some pushed toward the Colt band at the far end of the field and just stood there yelling. No words, just yelling.

Others hungry for pieces of the goal posts, big clusters of fans, showing only a spot of flailing fists at their center, marked the struggle for each big piece of post.

Shortly afterward, smaller clusters marked the scraps over smaller scraps, some of them as small as pocket size.

The battle of the goal posts was nearly over when it reached the point at which one young fellow ran out of a pileup yelling, "I got some, I got some!"

He was holding up his index finger and pointing to a precious peg, shouted, "It was the greatest."

Goal Posts Demolished

But while the goal posts were finally demolished, the stadium still stood, and the Baltimoreans set to work to shake it as much as their thousands of lungs could manage.

The team band, led by major-size, sized than ever, marched down the field trailing thousands of yellow, then swung in a very rough pounding movement, and stormed back up—and back and forth some more.

Among the more conservative

(Continued, Page 16, Column 3)

YULE ROAD TOLL MOUNTS TO 577

Rate Increases Rapidly As Motorists Return Home

Chicago, Monday, Dec. 29 (AP)—The holiday death toll at 1 A.M. this morning as compiled by the Associated Press:

Traffic.........577
Fires............91
Miscellaneous...92
_____
total...........760

Chicago, Dec. 28 (AP) — The homeward rush of Christmas vacationers today sent the country's death toll surging toward a pre-holiday estimate of 620.

Millions of autos jammed roads and generally good weather invited high speeds, one of the major factors in the bloody highway slaughter.

In a statement, the National Safety Council said, "Only the greatest care by motorists could hold the death toll down to our estimates."

The Council added, however, that only an unusual upswing in the death rate (in the week's) closing hours would bring the toll close to the all-time record of 706 traffic deaths set in the four-day 1936 Christmas holiday.

A heavy toll of casualties at the start of this Christmas holiday posed the possibility a new record would be set.

Multiple death smashups studded the toll of highway accidents.

In Illinois, four lives were snuffed out early today when one motorist sought to pass another on a hill in fog and collided with an oncoming car.

Four Milwaukee men were killed near Racine, Wis., and a fifth was injured today when their car plowed through a construction barricade.

The National Safety Council predicted before the holiday that the auto death toll would be 620

COULDN'T LET TEAM DOWN

Myhra Thought Tying Kick Would Be Good

By EDWIN H. BRANDT
[Sun Staff Correspondent]

New York, Dec. 28 — "I couldn't let these guys down, If I got a good snap and hold, I thought it would go through."

It was Steve Myhra talking above the noise of the Colt dressing room as a milling crowd desperately sought elbow room among the players, coaches, photographers, reporters, trainers, equipment and benches of the suddenly small room.

Gino Marchetti lay stretched out on a table, his broken right ankle in a cast, the game had clutched under one arm. The players wandered around, some what subdued and dazed except for Johnny Sample, who was chanting, "we are the best in the world. We are the best in the world."

Not Aware Of Time

Web Ewbank whirled around in the arms of Don Kellett and Carroll Rosenbloom and Mayor D'Alesandro, red-faced and puffing, shouted, "It was the greatest," as he said, "It was the greatest."

It was the greatest.

Myhra congratulated Marchetti, and shouted over his shoulder, "I knew we were pretty shy of time, but I didn't know at the goal posts were. No time, it was only nine seconds." He was talking about his 20-yard field goal, which sent the game into overtime and on into a 23-to-17 Colt victory.

It was Myhra's most important kick in his life, and about all he could do was grin for a while, at a loss for words.

"I knew it was the big one

(Continued, Page 16, Column 3)

DEFEAT GIANTS, 23-17, AS AMECHE SCORES IN SUDDEN-DEATH PERIOD

Myhra's Field Goal With Nine Seconds To Go In Regulation Game Ties Score, 17-17; Berry Breaks Playoff Record

Full page of pictures and other news of Colt victory . . . . Pages 13, 16, 17 and 26

By CAMERON C. SNYDER
[Sun Staff Correspondent]

New York, Dec. 28—Six years of sweat and frustration bore fruit today as the Colts stormed 80 yards in thirteen plays to win the National Football League championship, 23 to 17, in a sudden-death playoff with the New York Giants at Yankee Stadium.

Propelled by John Unitas's passes and Raymond Berry's catches, the Colts forced the game into the first sudden death extra period in pro history when Steve Myhra kicked a 20-yard field goal with nine seconds left in the regulation time.

Placekick Ties Score At 17-17

That placement evened the game at 17-17 and gave the Colts their winning chance, which Alan Ameche cashed on a 1-yard scoring plunge after 8.15 minutes had elapsed in the sudden-death period.

The first team to score in a sudden-death period is the winning team, no matter how the score is achieved.

Actually the Colts almost allowed the title to slip through their fingers, much to the dismay of 16,000 Baltimore rooters and the delight of a larger New York crowd composing a surprising attendance of 64,185. Pre-game forecasts had predicted a capacity gathering of 70,000-plus.

Helped By Strong Defense

It was only the cold, calculating and deadly play-calling of Unitas, and the clutch catching of Berry, who set a championship game record with twelve receptions, that brought the Colts back from what would have been a dismal and disappointing defeat.

This pair, augmented by a stout offensive line and the likes of L. G. Dupre, Ameche and Lenny Moore were just too much for the Giants. Fortified with luck and a burning desire after their defensive unit had staged a magnificent goal-line stand in the third period, the New Yorkers struck twice within the space of five minutes to pull ahead of the Colts.

Giants Trail In Statistics

Until their defense ignited the rest of their team, the Giants were appearing completely outclassed as the smoother functioning Colts compiled an overwhelming statistical edge.

But a team that has thrived on adversity during its entire pro history, dating back to 1947 in the old All-American Conference, and recently in 1953 when present management took over, thrived on adversity this time.

After the Colts blew their half-time lead of 14-3, they rose to their greatest heights behind Unitas.

Unitas raced the clock in the last minutes of the regulation time and won.

Trailing, 17-14, the Colts got possession of the ball with just 2 minutes and 25 seconds left and some 80 yards away from the promised land.

It was enough time, but just enough. Unitas passed and passed again. His first two were incomplete and only 1 minute and 50 seconds were left. He hit Moore for an important first down on the Colt 25, missed another, and then Berry became the target to the 50.

Giants Win Extra-Period Toss

Another Berry connection ate the ball was on the Giant 35 with 43 seconds left and time running.

It was Berry again on a diving catch to the 13. Fifteen seconds were on the clock as the Colt place-kicking unit lined up for the most important kick in Baltimore football history. Myhra, from the hills of North Dakota, a cool customer under tremendous pressure, lifted the pigskin and the Colts tied the sudden-death period.

It wasn't over. The game was just tied. The captains came out for the important coin-flipping ceremonies. The Giants were represented by Kyle Rote and Bill Svoboda, the Colts by Unitas, subbing for the injured Gino Marchetti.

Luck was with the giants again. They won the toss and

1958 WORLD CHAMPION BALTIMORE COLTS

LEFT TO RIGHT:
BOTTOM ROW: Coach Charles Winner, Carl Taseff, Art Spinney, Jackie Simpson, Ray Brown, Art DeCarlo, Lenny Moore, Bert Rechichar, L. G. Dupre, Billy Pricer, Trainer Ed Block
SECOND ROW: Trainer Dick Spassoff, Gino Marchetti, George Shaw, Jack Call, Ray Krouse, Steve Myhra, Leo Sanford, Alex Sandusky, John Sample, Don Shinnick, Head Coach Webb Ewbank
THIRD ROW: Coach Herman Ball, Bill Pellington, Raymond Berry, Leonard Lyles, Andy Nelson, Alan Ameche, Fred Thurston, George Preas, Don Joyce, Milt Davis, Equip. Mgr. Fred Schubach, Jr.
TOP ROW: Coach Bob Shaw, Jim Mutscheller, Sherman Plunkett, Ordell Braase, Madison Nutter, Gene Lipscomb, Jim Parker, John Unitas, Dick Szymanski, Art Donovan, Coach John Bridgers

Aggressive and alert, these five mobile linemen gave the Colts outstanding defensive play in 1958—1959. Left to right are Ordell Braase, Don Joyce, Gene "Big Daddy" Lipscomb, Art Donovan and Gino Marchetti.

It looks crowded out there and it is, as the opposition discovered when it tried to penetrate the Colts secondary in 1958-1959. Left to right are halfback Milt Davis, linebacker Don Shinnick, safetyman John Sample, linebacker Dick Szymanski, safetyman Andy Nelson, linebacker Bill Pellington and halfback Carl Taseff.

Offensive tackle George Preas was one of 12 rookies who made the Colts in 1955, which was the pivotal year in changing from an also-ran team to a contender and then a champion.

Jim Parker anchored the Colts' offensive line for 11 years, was All-Pro 8 times and was elected to Pro Football's Hall of Fame in 1973.

*Defensive back Carl Taseff is hoisted to the
shoulders of quarterback Johnny Unitas (19) and
halfback Ray Brown (17) as the happy Colts
celebrated in the dressing room after winning the
Westen Conference Division championship by
walloping the Los Angeles Rams, 45-26. Taseff
scored the final touchdown by scooping up a Ram
field goal attempt on the one-yard line and racing
99 yards. At left is halfback Lenny Moore.*

Colts Romp Rams, 45-26

Bring On The Giants!

See Column 7

Pimlico Charts . . . Page 6-S

Baltimore American

SECTION S
Sunday, Dec. 13, 1959

SPORTS

John F. Steadman
SPORTS EDITOR SAYS:

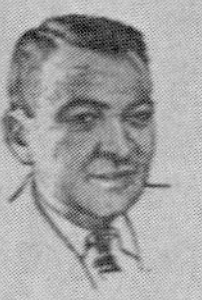

Colts Said It Could Be Done

LOS ANGELES—They crawled up the steep side of the mountain in a hand-over-hand climb. One mistake and they'd tumble back under an avalanche of Chicago Bears and San Francisco 49ers and probably never be heard from again.

But they reached their destination. They arrived. They made it all the way. Right this minute they repose on a high peak of success and are in no hurry to come back to level ground.

What the Baltimore Colts promised themselves and you, too, back on November 8, they have accomplished. The Western Conference championship of the National Football League is again their cherished prize and exclusive property.

Every football team and individual athlete aspires to do something like this but, unfortunately, few ever do. It was a courageous, come-from-behind journey.

The scoreboard told the bare results: Colts, 45; Los Angeles Rams, 26. But there was more determination, desire and personal application put forth in the story of the Baltimore conquest than mere words will ever convey.

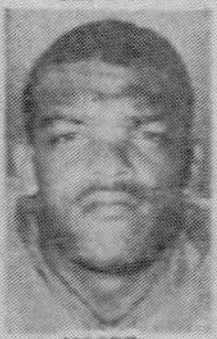

MOORE

Now to harken back to the darkest day in Baltimore since the great fire blackened the heavens in 1904 and smoke enveloped a depressed city. November 8 was the sad occasion when the Colts had been ground into the turf at Griffith Stadium by the Washington Redskins and the faint-of-heart said it was all over.

Baltimore had put on an inept, lack-of-aggressiveness performance in losing to the Redskins, 27-24. The Colts were "all done," some of their critics complained, and all but stuck a fork in them.

Put It In Writing

The record, after the Redskin upset, was a lackluster 4 and 3. The Colts were in second place behind the front-running 49ers, who had a two game lead and looked as solvent as money in the bank.

But right there the Colts, who obviously weren't talking for their own edification, said, we'll win the next five." Lenny Moore even put it in writing. He wrote a special story for the News-Post and said, without qualification, that the Colts would win all their remaining games and erase the 49ers' lead.

Tackle Ray Krouse, quarterback John Unitas and the rest of the Colts nodded in agreement. Well, they bounced back the way they said they would. They got up off the floor, these pride-wounded champions, and started to spar for time.

First, it was Green Bay which felt the "kick" of the retaliating Colts. Then came Los Angeles and San Francisco, back to back, in the final four games of the season. The Colts lined them up in their gunsights one at a time and squeezed the trigger. The end result: five wins in a row and Baltimore, once again, has established itself as one of the finest football teams in National League history.

How Now, Coach Howell

Jim Lee Howell, the New York Giant coach, was enthusiastic enough last August in Dallas, after the Colts had handled his team, 28-3, to call the Colts "the greatest of all time." Howell will get a further opportunity to appraise and praise the Colts Dec. 27 in Baltimore when the same two teams, which met for the title last year, come together again.

The Colts resented it last Nov. 8 when the quick-quitters in the press box and the grandstand detached themselves from the bandwagon, threw up their hands and said it "couldn't be done." But the Colts showed them. They even spelled it out.

But the Colts came all the way back and won like a champion should. They ventured out to the West Coast for the last two games with the Rams and 49ers. In 22 previous attempts, dating back to 1947, they had won only two games—both here in Los Angeles, once against the old Dons, and in 1954, a one-point win over the Rams.

They had to do it the hard way. The 49ers were knocked off a week ago and then here on Saturday the Rams got the same kind of treatment.

The Colts wanted to win this one and eliminate all chances of a playoff with the Bears and 49ers. Again, they got what they were after. Physically battered and fatigued, the Colts had a hard time

Turn to Page 3-S, Column 1.

Santa Couldn't Aid Rams

By VINCE BAGLI
Sunday American Staff Writer

LOS ANGELES—They were handing out transistor radios for Christmas when we got to the Ram dressing room shortly after the Colts had buried Los Angeles 45-26.

But even Santa Claus in this Gracious spirit of the coming Yuletide couldn't cut through the gloom of the hour.

"Do you think Eddie Erdelatz would be a good coaching selection?" we asked. (Sid Gillman had resigned just before the kickoff, effective with the final gun.)

"How do we know what Erdelatz would do? We need a man with an iron hand who knows the pro game. Sid (Gillman) is a genius, but we need somebody who won't listen so much to others and will put into practice what he thinks best," said a Ram lineman.

When asked what the future holds for him, Gillman replied, tensely, and yet politely, "I have no immediate plans." Sid had one more year to go on his contract.

Gillman sat, his chin in the palm of his hand, in the movie room beneath the big stadium. It was almost pathetic to see the players come through, and almost to the man, utter the same words, "We're sorry coach, that we didn't do a better job for you."

Not all stopped however, so you had to assume that this wasn't an unanimous effort to "win the last one for Sid."

"If you have all of this talent and still lose, whose fault is it?" asked another Ram, more disturbed about the loss to the Colts, than about the loss of the coach.

"You know it's possible to have too much talent don't you," he continued. "Look at Joe Marconi, he's a real good football player, but he sat on the bench for much of the year while they tried to justify that Matson trade.

"We like Ollie, but we gave up a lot of good players to get him and make our strong point, ball carrying, stronger."

"This team won't improve by being ripped apart, but we will get better if they balance things a little," he concluded.

THE RAMS were less than pleased with the work of Bill Downes' officiating crew, and actually bitter about the Colts scoring 28 points while gaining only 54 yards in the second half.

"Those guys (officials) gave them the go-ahead touchdown early in the fourth quarter and this knocked the heart out of our defensive unit, replied one of the disgruntled Rams.

Other Rams gave credit to the Colts for "playing well

Turn to Page 2-S, Column 8.

Mix Talks With Colts

LOS ANGELES—Tackle Ron Mix, the Baltimore Colts' first draft choice from the University of Southern California, met with team officials here Saturday for a preliminary discussion but did not sign a contract. Colt officials said they expected that Mix, after due deliberation, would sign.

His negotiating rights in the rival American Football League are held by the Boston franchise but the Los Angeles Chargers also admit they are interested in signing him.

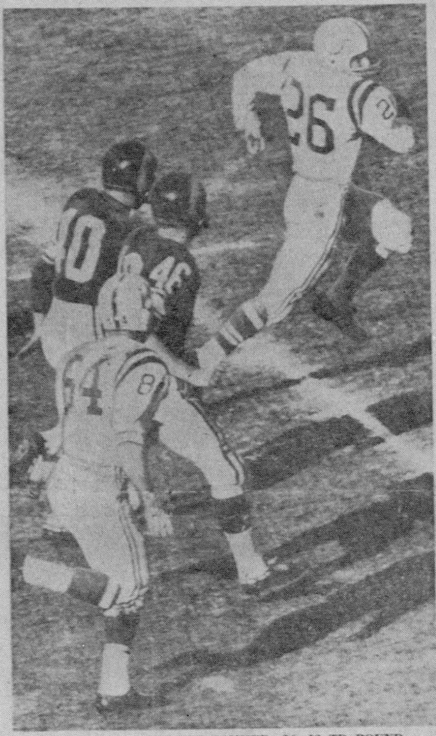

COLT HALFBACK MIKE SOMMER, 26, IS TD BOUND
. . . see sequence of his 53-yard scamper on Page 2-S.
—AP Wirephoto.

Wear Mantle Humbly

Little Celebration!

By ART JANNEY
American Sports Editor

LOS ANGELES—The mighty Baltimore Colts wear the mantle of a champion humbly and appreciatively.

And also with an immense amount of pride.

The Colts reacted to the winning of their second straight Western Division title in a business-like manner. There was, surprisingly, little celebration in the dressing room at Los Angeles Coliseum after they beat the Rams, fans and the well advertised California sun.

Of course, there were glad hands and broad smiles as the victorious but battered Hosses shed their football gear and had their wounds dressed.

BUT THERE was no hilarity of any kind, which is in marked contrast to last year in Baltimore when the Colts clinched their first divisional championship ever with a win over the Forty-Niners even before coming west.

This time they did it the hard way, with their fifth straight and title-clinching triumph over a charged-up band of Ram slammers in the final game of their regular schedule. But that's the hallmark of a real champion.

Upon reaching the dressing room here Saturday they knelt in prayer with their coaches.

"We have much to be thankful for," said coach Weeb Ewbank and this echoed the statements of his entire team.

On their way to the showers, there was an organized and lusty hooray. But that was it.

ACTUALLY, well wishers were more excited than the Colts.

Perhaps the Baltimorians had

Turn to Page 2-S, Column 5.

It's Official: Our Hosses Face Giants

By N. P. CLARK
Sunday American Staff Correspondent

LOS ANGELES—Okay, everybody stop worrying. Knock off gnawing those fingernails and have a beer. It's official.

In one of their most fantastic explosions yet, the Colts unloaded 21 stunning points in four minutes, 40 seconds of the fourth quarter before 65,528 new believers here Saturday to swamp the Rams 45-26 and nail for Baltimore its second straight Western Division NFL championship.

This was winning form at its bewildering, versatile best as the Steeds mixed up defensive and offensive brilliance in a dose of untakable proportions for the doughtly but doomed-to-dismay Rams.

The astonishing final period is the key illustration. In almost breath-taking succession it saw Johnny Unitas' nine-yard scoring pass to Jerry Richardson, Dick Syzmanski's 15-yard gallop to a payoff with an interception and Carl Taseff's 99-yard runback to a touchdown from a missed Ram field goal.

How much else could happen in five brief minutes—especially coming in a wild burst to shatter almost unbelievably what had been three solid quarters of nip-and-tuck, hair-raising football in which the Rams, blithely undaunted after seven straight losses, had scrambled and fought to 26-24 lead on Lou Michaels' four field goals.

Those three-pointers—from 15, 19, 40 and 27 yards—may have been the answer to the Ram downfall, even more than the five Baltimore interceptions and the three touchdowns thrown by Unitas as Johnny ran his record-breaking season total to 32 aerial scores.

The kicks, though reliably true from the big end's toe, meant that the Rams were just not getting in there for the big goal line payoffs that count the most.

There's no denying, however, that Baltimore aerial thievery, potent throughout the year, turned the course of this vital battle as it has many another . . . all five coming in the devastating second half.

Bill Pellington, Don Shinnick, Szymanski, Johnny Sample and Marv Matuszak were the Colt interceptors. For Shinnick, a home town boy who often starred on this field for UCLA, it was his seventh of the season to tie Milt Davis (still another ex-Uclan) for club leadership. Sample's and Matuszak's were the first for each.

THE FIVE interceptions ran the Colts' seasonal total to 40,

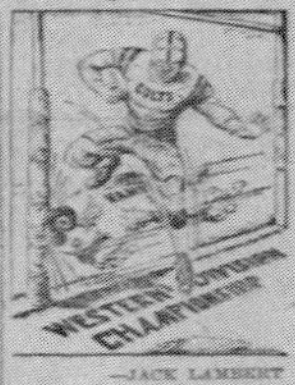

—JACK LAMBERT

just two short of the NFL record.

Taseff's long run, that finally broke Ram hearts beyond repair, did indeed tie a pro grid record. The 99-yard tour equalled a field goal runback performed in this same area by Jerry Williams, a 1951 Ram.

Raymond Berry, who caught two of Unitas' TD tosses, thus ran his 1959 total to 14 touchdowns, tying Lenny Moore's previous Colt highs for that many scores and 84 points.

Another electrifying Colt high spot was Mike Sommers' 53-yard touchdown run in the opening quarter to get Baltimore on the scoreboard for the first time after the home club had built up 10-0 advantage.

The ex-Redskin from G.W. has been a keen factor in the Steeds' racing finish to win their last five games after early season troubles following loss-

Turn to Page 2-S, Column 1.

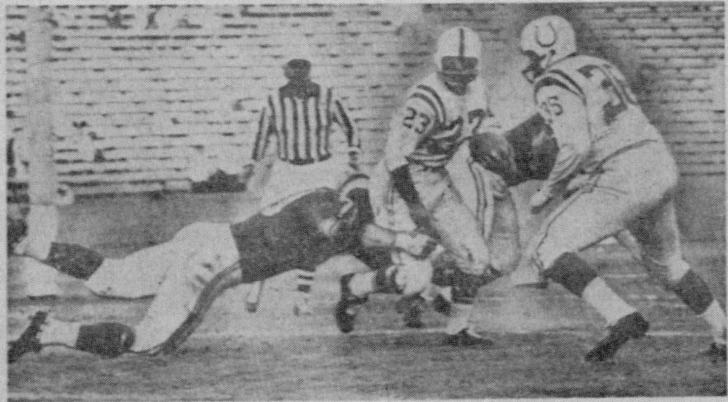

CARL TASEFF ELUDES GENE SELAWSKI NEAR START OF RECORD RUN
. . . Colt safetyman scooped up Ram attempted field goal and went 99 yards for td.

COLTS vs **GIANTS**

That's Andy Nelson (No. 80) in a foot race with Roosevelt Brown of the New York Giants as he returns an intercepted pass in the 1959 title game won by the Colts 31-16.

Steve Myhra shows his championship form again, this time in the 1959 Championship game. His holder is George Shaw.

95

Johnny Unitas is shown here rolling out of the pocket during action in the 1959 championship game. Blocking for him are George Preas (60) and Lenny Moore (24).

Sports—Local News
Classified Ads

THE SUN

Lancelotta Takes Lead
In Pin Tourney: Page 16

PAGE 15

BALTIMORE, MONDAY, DECEMBER 28, 1959

PAGE 15

....And Still Champions

HATS OFF TO COLTS — A hat soars through the air like a jet propelled rocket as jubilant Colt fans celebrate their team's 31-to-16 victory over the Giants. A few wild fans begin tearing down the goal posts for souvenirs.

FIELD GENERAL CONFERS — John Unitas checks with officials on first down measure-

Gifford Raps Sample For 'Just Yapping'

By CAMERON C. SNYDER

Jim Lee Howell, New York Giant coach was smiling and affable in the dressing room after his team lost its second straight championship game with the Colts.

He was disappointed, no doubt about that, but none of the bitterness he must have felt colored his good manners of the game.

But Howell is cut from the old cloth. Frank Gifford, the matinee idol of the Giants, didn't hold back or try to hide his feelings.

Howell Praises Fans

When asked what Johnny Sample had said to him just a few plays before the Colt safetyman had picked off a Giant pass and sped to a touchdown, Gifford growled.

"He was just yapping. He rapped all through the game. Exsionally do. They haven't acquired that little bit of class."

Howell couldn't say enough about the conduct of the Colt fans. "They behaved admirably after they were incited by a newspaper article.

"I expected the worst but the fans didn't drown out our quarterback. In fact, they should be congratulated for their sportsmanship. They here much better than

Sports Index

Evening Sun bowling	Page 16
Racing selections, cards	Page 16
Sandlot results	Page 17
Colt picture page	Page 18
Other Colt news	Pages 19, 20
Morning After	Page 20
Other football	Page 20
Bullets win	Page 21

our fans in a game this year with the Cleveland Browns."

About his strategy of attempting a fourth down running play instead of a field goal from the Colt 27 late in the third quarter, Howell said:

"When we are deep in the other team's territory and need just a foot or so, we'll always go for it. Field goals help, but touchdowns are what you need to win.

Colt Offensive Questioned

"That was the turning point for us, but we weren't as sharp as I had hoped we would be. I'm not trying to detract from the Colts when I say that, "Howell rumbled on to say, "they had a lot to do with it, particularly defensively.

"I didn't think the Colt offensive was real sharp, not as sharp as I expected. Now I know that must

(Continued, Page 19, Column 4)

SAMPLE OF THINGS TO COME — Colt Halfback John Sample, who made two interceptions in final quarter, returns a punt in second period, as Giants' Joe Biscaha closes in.

meet on Giants' 4 in fourth period. The Colt moved by inches but scored on the next play

This picture of John Unitas, cradled in the arms of Steve Myhra, left, and Carl Taseff, following the 1959 title conquest, was carried in newspapers all over the country and brought Unitas strong mail reaction. Some high school coaches thought he was giving a bad example to youngsters by holding a beer bottle. But it was gingerale and the company later gave Unitas his first major endorsement because of the publicity the photo received.

1959 WORLD CHAMPION BALTIMORE COLTS

TOP: Dave Sherer, Jerry Richardson, Gino Marchetti, Sherman Plunkett, Jim Parker, Gene (Big Daddy) Lipscomb, George Preas, Madison (Buzz) Nutter, Art Donovan, Dick Szymanski.
SECOND: Asst. Coach Don McCafferty, Leo Sanford, Don Shinnick, Andy Nelson, Don Joyce, Lenny Moore, Art Spinney, Alex Sandusky, Ray Krouse, Ordell Braase, Asst. Coach John Sandusky.
THIRD: Asst. Trainer Dick Spasoff, Asst. Coach Herman Ball, Alan Ameche, Bill Pellington, Steve Myhra, Jim Mutscheller, Milt Davis, Johnny Unitas, Ray Brown, Marv Matuszak, Johnny Sample, Ray Berry, Charley Winner, Coach Weeb Ewbank.
BOTTOM: Equip. Mgr. Fred Schubach, Jr., Art DeCarlo, Hal Lewis, Billy Pricer, Carl Taseff, Alex Hawkins, Jackie Simpson, L.G. Dupre, Bert Rechichar, Trainer Ed Black

A very popular head coach for seven years was Don Shula who compiled a fabulous record of 75-26-4.

CHAPTER FIVE
PAIN & HEARTBREAK

Sustaining success is the most trying challenge in sports. And so it was to be with the two-time champion Colts. They were on their way to qualifying for a third straight title in 1960 when they won a bruising battle against the Bears, 24-20, but subsequently lost all the rest of their games. The objectives of winning the division and retaining the crown ebbed away. After back-to-back championships, the title changed hands. Things were going to be different.

Thus, it was a long interval when the Colts were more than a representative kind of a team but the uncontrollable variables, injuries and the harsh breaks of the game, caught up with them . . . the same as it does to all clubs. The 1960 campaign, with hopes so alive and optimistic, suddenly flattened out and the Colts fell to third place with a 6-6 overall record. Berry and Mutscheller had knee problems, which restricted their passing game, and a 10-3 loss to the Rams found Unitas' streak of 47 consecutive games throwing touchdown passes come to an end. He wasn't at all upset because his own statistics never got his personal attention, only the scoreboard result.

Berry came off knee surgery for 1961 but still caught 75 passes. Unitas had what might be considered a minor problem to the uninitiated but it resulted in major difficulties, especially for a quarterback. He jammed the middle finger of his passing hand, which meant he had to primarily grip the ball with only three fingers and thumb. Still he played, even though his performance was considerably effected. He couldn't get the true feel of the ball, the same as it would have been for a concert pianist trying to touch the keys.

The Colts were 6-6 in 1960, 8-6 in 1961 and had another .500 year in 1962, after Moore cracked his knee-cap in an exhibition in Pittsburgh. There was a game in 1962, to illustrate the way the Colts' luck was going, when they outgained the Green Bay Packers 380 yards to 116, had 19 first downs to eight and possessed the ball for 30 more plays, 79 to 49, and still they lost, 17-13.

Starting the season, a "day" was held for Arthur Donovan, who retired at the suggestion of Ewbank. Donovan was 37, had played 12 years in the NFL and was a much beloved figure in Baltimore. The Colts' organization couldn't participate in the honors because it didn't want to establish a precedent and have to be involved in all future retirements.

Donovan had gone to training camp in 1962 and soon got the message. He was being used less all the time and, finally, at Kellett's urging, they had a meeting to plan his leaving the Colts. "Before I do anything, I want to tell the best friend I have in this town," said Donovan. He called this writer from Kellett's club basement, explained what had happened and then cried like a baby, a 6-foot-3, 265 pound "baby" who was tough physically but softly sentimental.

The "Donovan Day" was held before the Colts' opener with the Rams. It was put on by a committee headed by Bob Robertson, who suggested the idea; Lou Grasmick who handled the staging; Morris Kasoff, Jim Lindsay, Joe Clifford and 35 others. All the funds were raised by the committee via volunteer contributions. It resulted in the presentation of a Cadillac automobile, a set of golf clubs from pro Johnny Bass at Pine Ridge and numerous other gifts that showed the city's esteem for Donovan. Jim Mutscheller, a retiring teammate, also was on the committee. He worked hard. Nothing similar was done for him but he realized Donovan was something special and, besides, Mutscheller was never self-centered. He was elated Donovan was given such warm, tender treatment.

Donovan didn't want to wear a uniform but Grasmick insisted he do it. "Without the uniform he would have been obscure on the field. It added luster," explained Grasmick, who was striving for a dramatic occasion.

In his emotional acceptance of the accolades and presents, Donovan thanked the public and choked everybody when he said over the public address system, "Up in Heaven there is a lady who is happy the City of Baltimore was so good to her son — a kid from the Bronx." Then he trotted off the field, leaving a crowd of 54,796 in tears, too.

The Colts, as a team, had leveled-off. Faces were changing, the normal transition. But three seasons without a championship disenchanted Rosenbloom and there was talk of Ewbank being replaced as head coach.

Ewbank, though, was confident he'd be retained. He learned of his firing when he returned from the Senior Bowl in Mobile. Odd, but hadn't it been at the Senior Bowl in 1954 when Kellett first talked to him about coming to the Colts? Now he came back to Baltimore from a coaching assignment believing he was still the man in charge but his regime had ended, showing a total of 59 wins, 52 defeats and one tie. He had given professional organization to the Colts on the field. It was a team fundamentally sound, playing contemporary football but wasn't

101

A covey of Colts converge on top of Ram running back Dick Bass. From left to right are Bill Pellington, John Sample, Don Shinnick and Jim Welch.

winning as often as Rosenbloom desired.

The new coach was Don Shula, a Colts' alumnus. When the Colts' veterans, mainly Gino Marchetti and Bill Pellington, realized Ewbank was going to be dropped and were asked what they thought about a replacement they answered with one unified voice...Shula, who was then a 33-year-old assistant with the Detroit Lions. Shula was destined to be a successful coach and the Colts knew it. When he was a defensive halfback in earlier years, there were occasions when he actually "coached" the coaches. He had been a student of the game, was an excellent tackler and all-out competitor.

It was a continuation of the same injury bugaboo under Shula as it was with Ewbank. Berry was out five weeks with a shoulder ailment and Lenny Moore hurt his head, complaining of "buzzing sounds". The Colts won eight, lost six but Tom Matte, then in his third year, showed he could play and two rookies, tackle Bob Vogel and end John Mackey, were impressive. Not a bad start for a freshman head coach.

Shula, in his second year with the Colts, fared even better. His team put together a streak of eleven straight, longest in club history, as Moore blistered the goal line for 20 touchdowns and won "Comeback Player of the Year". Shula was named "Coach of the Year" and Alex Hawkins gained his first notoriety as the infamous "Captain Who". Shula designated Hawkins, the leader of the special team, as one of the co-captains for the pre-game introductions and he wasn't exactly what you would call well known. So he became "Captain Who", a role he enjoyed and played to the hilt.

A "day" was held in honor of the retiring Pellington and Marchetti so, like Donovan before him, the Colts were undergoing defensive changes. The West was won by a 24-7 blasting of the Rams as the defense rushed Roman Gabriel and Bill Munson off their feet and sacked them eleven times. This brought the Colts to another coveted title show-down, against the Browns in Cleveland, where Shula had played at John Carroll University and later with the Browns.

The Colts were highly favored but at halftime it was 0-0. The Browns found and exploited a weakness in the Colts' secondary in the final half. They hit for 17 points in the third period and went on to rip the Colts 27-0.

Frank Rayan threw three scoring passes to Gary Collins of 18, 42 and 51 yards. That combination was devastating. The Colts had no excuses and offered none. They had been hammered.

It had been the "year of the bugle", for this writer. Earlier in the season, a group of enthusiastic fans calling themselves the "Bugle Boys of Baltimore", were told they were going to be barred from the Stadium if they persisted in bringing their bugles.

We took a strong stand in their behalf and got them playing again. As a reward, they named us an honorary member of the "Bugle Boys".

A visiting publicity man, Art Johnson, of the San Francisco 49ers, was in Baltimore to publicize an appearance of his team, read about the controversy and was so amused he went to a hock shop on Baltimore Street and bought an old Army bugle. He presented it as a surprise gift and we played at the games, blowing it in the press box and frequently over the radio when we served as a color man. The bugle finally was "buried at sea" under the Chesapeake Bay Bridge, in a mock funeral off the stern of a fishing boat, as Norman Almony, Chuck Thompson, Herb Cahan and friends observed the ceremony. We felt the bugle had more than served its purpose and should be given an honorable end to its long hard career.

The Colts were naturally embarrased by their demise in Cleveland and it took some restraint for the world's worst bugle player not to sound taps when it was over. But there's always next year and 1965 was to be another productive showing. It was capped with a bitter and controversial defeat by the Green Bay Packers after both teams tied for divisional honors with identical 10-3 and 1 marks.

Two of the losses were sustained in successive weeks to the Bears and Packers. First Unitas injured his knee and was sidelined in a cast. Then his replacement, Gary Cuozzo, suffered a shoulder separation. So the Colts were completely wiped out at quarterback. It was too late in the year to find another and get him ready. So Shula, always one to make the best of a bad situation, decided he would try Matte at QB. It required changing the entire offensive philosophy but Shula didn't stand around feeling sorry for himself. He never has and never will.

Matte had been a split-T QB at Ohio State but was more a runner than a passer. So that was how Shula used him. Against the Rams, in the season finale, Matte carried 16 times from the QB slot and gained 99 yards as the Colts won 20-17, the difference being a 50-yard field goal by Lou Michaels. This brought the Colts and Packers together for a playoff for the Western Division. The Packers had walloped the Colts earlier, the day Cuozzo was injured, 45-27, on an occasion when Hornung scored five touchdowns in Baltimore, despite the presence of a crowd of 60,238 and the encouragement it created.

The Colts, lacking a QB to run a normal offense, had to be content with ball control. Bart Starr was injured on the first series when he was hit with a crushing tackle. But Zeke Bratkowski came in for Starr and the "old pro" didn't slow the Packers at all, but still they couldn't move against the aggressive Baltimore defense, which had scored early when Don Shinnick recovered a fumble.

*Considered one of the premier pass receivers
in the history of the game, Raymond Berry
shows us in this group of photographs why he was
elected into the Hall of Fame in 1973. In thirteen
seasons with the Colts, Berry caught 631 passes for
9275 yards and 68 touchdowns.*

The Colts continued on top, 10-7, with only 1:58 to play. They were about to pull off the most improbable feat imaginable, winning the division and getting to play for the championship with a converted halfback at quarterback. But here's where things went wrong all over again. Only a scant 1:58 was on the clock when Chandler, who had been on the losing side in the Giants' two title losses to the Colts in 1958 and 1959, tried a tying field goal from the 27 yard line. The snap, the kick and it was sliced to the right, higher than the post. Chandler's reaction was to shake his head, like a man who had just missed a short putt in golf for all the money.

But one official under the goal post, Jim Tunney, raised his arms to signal it was good. Michaels, Shinnick and Fred Miller, among others, offered heated protest. So, instead of the Colts winning, 10-7, and going home they were tied and faced with sudden death. Deep into the extra period, at 13:39, another field goal, this one from 25 yards away, was good for a Packer win, 13-10. There was no complaint with that call but the earlier one set off a raging controversy. Had it been called no good, the Colts would have had the ball and probably been able to hold on for a 10-7 win.

A steady performer on defense and nifty return specialist was Lenny Lyles who holds the Colts single game kickoff return record with 202 yards against the 49ers in 1960.

106

The controversial decision loomed large in the post-game reactions. We were fortunate to get a clip of the film from an out-of-town source we have never identified. The NFL was more than curious but wasn't able to find out how we secured it. We took the segment to WBAL-TV and asked Pete Greer, a veteran camerman, who had worked with movies most all his life, to screen it and analyze the angle of the ball in relation to the upright. Greer said the field goal wasn't any good and reaffirmed his opinion with constant slow-motion re-runs and then a meticulous frame-by-frame evaluation. Other photographers reacted the same way.

The pictures were printed in *The News American* and the controversy boiled again. The league office had to stand behind Tunney. It was an honest error, made near the end of an all-out competitive battle between two of football's finest teams. But still a costly mistake.

Spectators in the end-zone, all Packer partisans, also admitted the kick was bad. But the result could not be altered. The Packers took advantage of the highly disputed win and went on to the NFL crown, beating the Browns, 23-12.

The league decided the next season, after careful scrutiny of the pictures and pondering the situation, to place not one but two officials under the goal posts on field goal attempts and to rise the uprights ten feet. They were facetiously called the "Baltimore Extensions". They probably never would have been lengthened unless the incident had happened, despite the fact kickers were getting the ball higher and officials had to mentally draw an imaginery line to the sky from the top of the posts when the ball reached an altitude that exceeded the highest point of the upright.

It was a tough way for the Colts to go, losing on a

Bobby Boyd tops all Colt defensive backs with a career high 57 interceptions and return yardage of 994 yards. It appears here that he's about to pick off this pass intended for Detroit's Jim Gibbons.

bad field goal try, but the next season was traumatic in a different way. The Colts were riding high with a 7-2 showing, tied for first with the Packers, when Unitas, the "meal ticket", hurt his right shoulder and 1966 became a similar disappointment. The injury was sustained against the Falcons in Atlanta. Unitas continued to play even though he wasn't himself. He was far off form and Cuozzo was given more game action. The Colts dropped three of their last five and it was another second place finish. They had to watch on television as the Packers won over Dallas for the NFL crown and then defeated the Kansas City Chiefs, 35-10, in the first Super Bowl played.

It was getting ridiculous, a time when you started to wonder what could happen next to frustrate a team and its championship dream. Well, the Colts found still an entirely different set of circumstances abruptly denying their ambitions in 1967. It was an alteration in the playoff plan, dictated by the fact the league had pre-determined post-season dates

When Tom Matte came out of Ohio State and joined the Colts in 1961, he brought his helmet with him! Leading the interference in this action against the Bears are Wiley Feagin (61), Palmer Pyle (62), Jim Parker (77) and George Preas (60). Mark Smolinski is blocking the Bear's Joe Fortunato (31) while Doug Atkins (81) trails the play.

that had to be filled, without delaying the championship games in each conference and the Super Bowl. Yes, another cruel blow was about to hit them.

Everything was letter perfect...except the ending. This time, the Colts, with Unitas free of injuries, had an 11-1-2 showing, the same as the Rams, but got only the chance to take a long plane ride home from Los Angeles, realizing the season was over and they wouldn't be in any kind of a playoff. NFL rules decreed in the event of a tie the title would be decided by which team had scored the most points in meetings against each other. The Rams and Colts had deadlocked 24-24 in Baltimore but in Los Angeles, the final of the regular schedule, it was a 34-10 result.

Baltimore had the best offense in football, 5,008 yards, and the defense permitted the fewest number of points in club history. But still there wasn't going to be a playoff chance for the Colts, as good as they

Although there was no way to know it at the time, this was to be Weeb Ewbank's last training camp when this picture was taken in July of 1962. Surrounding Weeb as they review game films from the previous season are (l. to r.) Charlie Winner, Don McCafferty (who would succeed Don Shula in 1970), John Sandusky (who would replace McCafferty midway through the 1972 season) and Herman Ball.

were. Again, controversy ensued and the cry this time was titles should be decided on the field and not at some league meeting held in the off-season. The Colts were again bedeviled by a kick, this one by Bruce Gossett from the 47 yard line that had hit the goal post and slithered inside to help the Rams gain the 24-24 draw in mid-season. Had the ball bounced the other way, the Colts would have won the division but it wasn't to be.

Shula was wondering what he had to do for fortune to smile. On a deep personal matter he also lost one of his closest friends, Joe Campenella, who was a middle guard of the Colts when the team came from Dallas. Campanella had been appointed general manager of the Colts after Kellett's retirement following the 1966 season, but he hardly had a chance to function in the position. Joe died playing handball with Shula, only two blocks from Maryland General Hospital, when he suffered a heart seizure. Campanella and Shula were elated to be working together but it was all too brief.

Campanella's successor was Harry Hulmes, who had come to the Colts when this reporter left in 1958. A kind, gentle, considerate, honest and hard working individual, he got along well with everyone. Shula and Hulmes had a warm rapport and the combination wasn't broken up until 1970, when Hulmes left to go to the New Orleans Saints and Shula shortly thereafter resigned to take the coaching-general manager job with the Dolphins.

Hulmes had worked for the Baltimore Orioles in their first year, 1954, in the American League before going to Bucknell University as publicity director. An oddity occurred when the Orioles weren't sure if Hulmes or another young assistant, Harry Dalton, would be assigned to the business office or the farm department. Dalton was picked for the minor league operation and, ultimately, became a force in building the Orioles to world title status in 1966 as the club's personnel director.

The 1968 season continued along the same pattern, the Colts dominating the league, beating the Vikings, 24-14, in the playoff and then more than gaining revenge against the Browns, who had beaten them 27-0 in 1964, by wiping them out, 34-0. There was one stretch late in the season when the Colts failed to permit a touchdown in four straight games. It was necessary to go back to 1937 and the Giants to find when it had happened before.

Winning the championship of the league had always been what it is all about but that part of the elimination process had changed. It had come to be regarded as merely another step for a team to play in the Super Bowl. The Colts had, indeed, qualified.

Instead of a football game, the Super Bowl became an Ameican happening...a Roman-like holiday, a lavish extravaganza that offered gold and glory. Every team wanted to know the experience.

General manager Don Kellett and Don Shula display happy smiles on the signing of Shula's contract in January, 1963.

Alex Hawkins...Captain Who...prepares to make a spectacular game-winning catch against the Vikings in 1964. Alex enjoyed a strong popularity in Baltimore and later went on to be a broadcaster for CBS.

*Gino Marchetti (l.) and Bill Pellington (r.)
congratulate Don Shula after he was named Coach
of the Year in 1964.*

Don Shinnick came out of UCLA in 1957 and provided outstanding linebacking services for the next twelve years.

Gary Cuozzo could certainly have been a first string quarterback with just about any team in the NFL when he graduated from the University of Virginia in 1963. However, because of a man named Unitas, Gary remained a back-up with the Colts for four years. There were times, though, when the call for duty came as shown here against the Packers in 1965.

When both John Unitas and Gary Cuozzo were injured late in the 1965 season, halfback Tom Matte had to take over the controls at quarterback. Shown here is the wrist band that he wore to refer to for his play selection, which is now in the Pro Football Hall of Fame in Canton, Ohio.

This kick by Don Chandler (black arrow) of the Green Bay Packers became the most controversial play in the history of the Colts. The ball is shown going wide (as illustrated by the white arrow) of the upright but the official, Jim Tunney, under the goal post, called it good. Chandler reacted after the kick by turning his head in a dejected manner. The next season, the league extended the uprights and stationed two officials under the post. The disputed call enabled the Packers to tie the Colts, 10-10, and then win in overtime on another field goal that gave them the Western Division title and the chance to win the NFL crown.

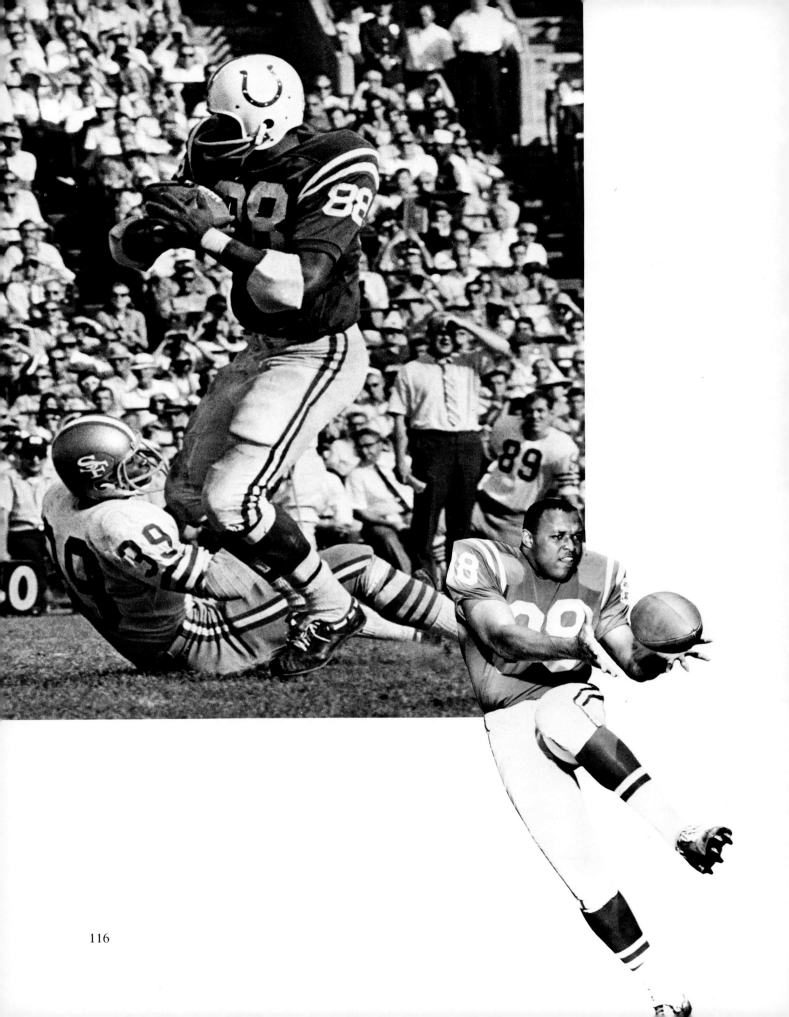

John Mackey was considered one of the toughest and most rugged tight ends in NFL history. These photos show why.

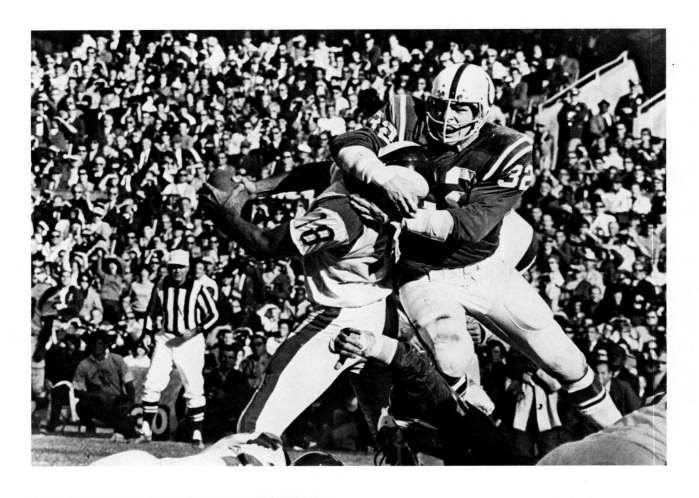

*Mike Curtis enjoyed a strong popularity in
Baltimore and was considered one of the most
fearless linebackers in league history.*

Jim O'Brien and Earl Morrall jump for joy just seconds after O'Brien's field goal split the uprights with seven seconds left on the clock to win Super Bowl V against the Cowboys, 16-13.

CHAPTER SIX
HORROR & HAPPINESS

It was one of those routine announcements, far from the kind that drew an eight-column newspaper headline. The Colts were picking up Earl Morrall from the New York Giants as a spare quarterback. It was ultimately agreed they would give the Giants a substitute tight-end named Butch Wilson in payment.

There was no way to foretell the part a seemingly obscure transaction, the acquisition of Morrall, was going to play in the Colts' immediate future. Shula wanted Morrall as a back-up to Unitas and obtained him only two weeks before the final exhibition, a date with the Cowboys in Dallas. They didn't have long to wait before they had to use him. Like right away.

Unitas was in the act of throwing a pass, was hit and almost had his arm slit away from the rest of him. He suffered a serious tear inside the right elbow and it was to impair his throwing motion and the amount of velocity he could put on the ball. So there was yet another unfortunate break exploding in their face as they got ready for the 1968 season.

It was a remarkable development, a saving action, that Morrall was there to assume command. Shula had come in personal contact with Morrall when they were both with the Lions, Shula as an assistant coach and Morrall as a quarterback. He knew the type of friendly personality Morrall was, how he could adjust to difficult situations, the sterling character of the man and how much he was underrated as a quarterback.

So the Colts had no alternative but to go with Morrall and hope the lame arm of Unitas would respond to treatment. It did but late in the year, at a time when Morrall had things going so good for the Colts that even a sound, productive Unitas could hardly have improved on the performance. Morrall quickly gained the respect of his teammates. He had a good arm, was cool under the gun and found the key to getting the Colts to the goal line was a full mix of the pass and run, plus a heavy assortment of play-action.

Morrall opened the season and won for the Colts against, as the schedule dictated, the team that originally owned him and had sent him away, the 49ers. He later lofted touchdown passes to Willie Richardson and Jimmy Orr and the Colts won, 26-0, over the New York Giants. It was a red-faced experience for the Giants, being taken apart so effectively by a quarterback that ony two weeks before the season started they decided they couldn't use.

Perhaps the most talented all-time duo at the safety positions were Rick Volk and Jerry Logan. Between the two of them, they hold a number of club interception records. Example: Most career interceptions returned for touchdowns — Jerry Logan with five; longest interception return — Rick Volk, 94 yards against Chicago in 1967. In this photo, both Volk (21) and Logan (20) go for the interception against the Cardinals.

It was to become one of Morrall's most magnificent seasons. He had been a No. 1 draft choice of the 49ers in 1956, the year the Colts had picked up Unitas as a free-agent. He was subsequently dealt to the Steelers, the Lions and then the Giants before the Colts let him take them to their first Super Bowl. Morrall was so outstanding he was voted "Player of the Year" in the NFL, an honor that had gone to Unitas only the year before. For some unexplained reason, Morrall had been written off as just another journeyman. This was grossly inaccurate and also unfair. But Morrall never had too many "highs" or "lows", and was similar to Unitas in that respect. He was a talkative type, much like an infielder in baseball hollering to encourage his mates between pitches. That was the way Earl was. "Okay, gang," he'd say, "we missed that time but three more downs to get them. Let's make this one good. Let's keep up the old hustle." And so it went.

In practice, the players enjoyed the way he was always telling himself in passing drills, "Okay, Earl, get it up, get it up". This was a reminder that he wanted to make sure he had his arm comng over the top and not from the side, where the ball could be blocked. Morrall's consistent performance was bringing attention from all over. He gave the Colts a superb effort and it wasn't until late in the schedule that Unitas got work in relief just to make sure if anything happened to Morrall he'd be ready. to provide the touch.

The Colts, with Morrall at the controls, won 13 of 14 games and demolished the Browns, 34-0, in Cleveland for the NFL title. It had only been four years before when they were put down, 27-0, on the same field. Matte had three touchdowns and averaged five yards per carry. Leroy Kelly, the NFL rushing leader with 1,239 yards, could only get 28 against the Colts' tough defense. So the Colts were ready for their first Super Bowl. It was to be played in the Orange Bowl at Miami and the Colts, being called one of the finest teams in NFL history, entered the game as 16 point favorites. They lost to the New York Jets, 16-7, to become the first NFL club to bow to an AFL representative. The over-confident Colts were as stunned as if the world had fallen off its axis or time stopped or hell had frozen over.

Earl Morrall took the Colts to one of their most successful seasons in 1968 with a regular season record of 13-1 and two playoff victories to win the NFL Championship. But then came Super Bowl III.....

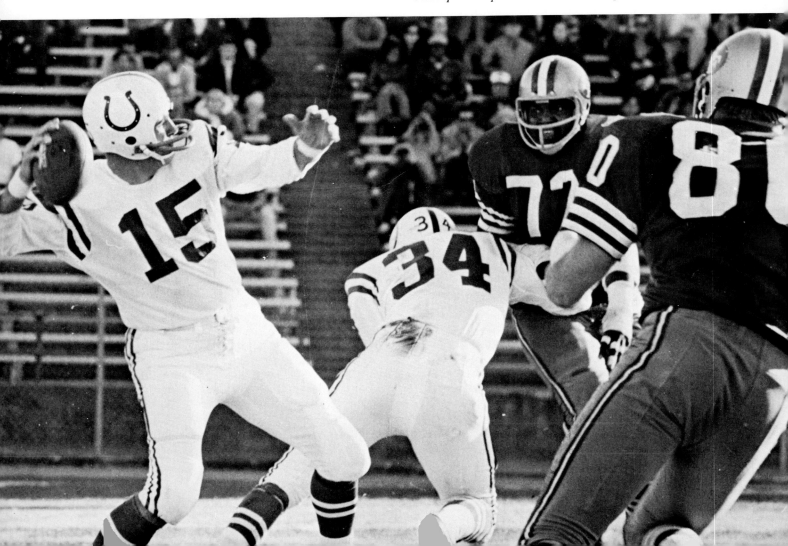

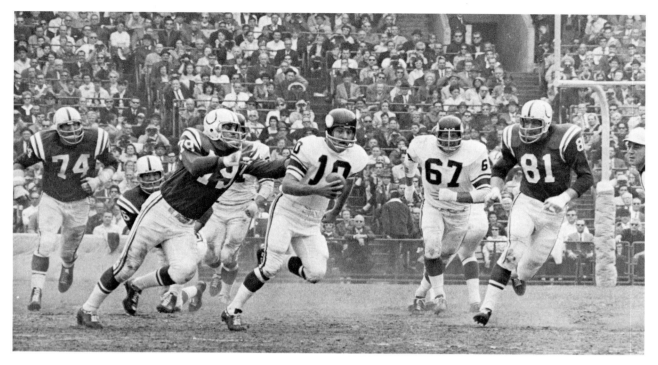

Lou Michaels was an excellent field goal kicker for six years (1964—69) and holds virtually every club record for field goals and points-after-touchdown. He also played a very steady and durable defensive end as he shows here during the 1968 Western Conference Championship game against Fran Tarkenton and the Vikings. The Colts won this one 24—14 before 60,238 fans at Memorial Stadium.

How could it have happened? They still don't know. No doubt, they had deceived themselves into believing an easy afternoon was coming up against the Jets. So they weren't ready. They thought they had a soft piece of cake. It wasn't that way at all and when the Jets led 7-0 at halftime, it gave the underdogs a feeling the Colts weren't as awesome as they had been described. The Jets, meanwhile, looked at each other, saw they were all still alive and breathing, plus leading in the game.

So why not go out and complete the job? They did. The first score had come after the Jets staged an 80-yard drive, Matt Snell reaching pay-dirt from the four yard line. All the other Jets' points, ten in all, came from the conversion by Jim Turner and then three field goals of 32, 30 and nine yards by the same kicker. Going into the fourth period, it was 16-0 and Morrall had come up with a cold hand. But the Colts weren't doing much offensively. Unitas came off the bench to take them to their

Quiet and unassuming in nature, Glenn Ressler proved to be a tough and dilligent guard throughout his 10 years of battle in the Baltimore trenches.

only score, Jerry Hill driving over from the one.

The Jets directed their attack away from linebacker Mike Curtis and went the other way, to the left side, where Ordell Braase was trying to hide an injury and Namath felt he could also exploit linebacker Don Shinnick and halfback Lenny Lyles. It was Namath, three nights before the game, who said he guaranteed the Jets were going to win. There was laughter and scorn but he helped make it happen. The Colts, in the early going, but only briefly, made it appear they were going to have an easy afternoon. They moved quickly but seemed to transmit the feeling they could score whenever they got ready so there was no real hurry. Such an attitude is usually fatal to an athlete, or a team, and it was to the Colts.

The Colts nearly scored before the end of the first half. Morrall made use of the "flea-flicker", a play Ewbank had dusted off in his early years with the Colts. It went all the way back to the era of the immortal Bob Zuppke at Illinois. But teams still use it from time-to-time, with variations.

Morrall handed off to Matte, who moved to the outside, and then quickly pulled up and tossed the ball back to Morrall. The intended receiver sprinting down the left sideline was Jimmy Orr. He was wide open but Morrall couldn't find him. It was as if Orr had vanished. So Morrall looked for someplace else to throw. He aimed for Jerry Hill over the middle but the Jets' secondary had time to get itself together and the ball was intercepted.

No explanation was ever given for what happened, except Morrall couldn't find Orr. It wasn't as if Jimmy headed for the men's room or stepped out to the nearest bar for a scotch and water. It's the belief of this observer that Orr's blue jersey blended in with a marching band of musicians that was headed for the end zone to perform at intermission. The backdrop was blue, the same color the Colts were wearing, and Morrall just couldn't pick-up the primary receiver. It was almost as if he was camouflaged.

Ordell Braase puts a head lock on Falcon halfback Junior Coffey as Rick Volk and Jerry Logan add assistance. Braase played for the 1958—1959 championship teams and was one of the most respected defensive ends in the league.

The Colts were stunned over what happened to them, losing to a foe virtually everyone agreed was inferior. One reporter in a pre-game prediction ventured a prophesy they'd win 55-0. The overwhelming feeling was it would be a rout, almost any score the Colts wanted to make it. This led to a swollen case of over-confidence. The Colts were ready to be had. And they were.

Much of the after-game second-guessing had to do with the way the Colts had prepared in the days leading up to the Super Bowl. Their wives and children were invited to join the team at the Galt Ocean Mile Hotel, located on the ocean, and the night before there was a dinner in an elegant restaurant for all to attend. Had the Colts beaten the Jets this would have been cited as the perfect way to relax a team for a major game. But the thought was introduced and unfortunately

Rugged Jerry Hill struggles and stretches to get the ball over the goal line against Dallas in this 1967 contest won by the Colts, 23-17.

perpetuated, to this day, that the Colts acted as though they were a bunch of Volunteer Firemen at a beach convention. The only fault to be found was in the end result. . .they didn't win.

The Colts had arrived in Fort Lauderdale on a Sunday, a full week before the game, and the players were free that night to do what they wanted. It was on that occasion when Lou Michaels went into a cocktail lounge and, wouldn't you know, encountered Namath. They talked in a friendly way but then Michaels got around to telling Namath how the Colts were going to tear them apart. Namath said the Jets were definitely going to show up and weren't afraid of the Colts' vaunted reputation. That's when Michaels, a fierce competitor, asked Namath if he wanted to step outside and he would give him a sample of what was going to happen. It was a direct physical

Quick-footed Willie Richardson gathers in a pass against the Redskins.

challenge. Namath side-stepped it and ordered another round of drinks. Had Namath gone outside with Michaels, it could have led to serious blood-shed. Joe would have probably wound up in a hospital and, possibly, been in no shape to play a game the following Sunday.

The Colts were shell-shocked after losing to the Jets. It was a bad dream. Make-believe. They continued to tell themselves it didn't happen, or that they wanted a recount or the chance to go out right then to play it over. They were numb Sunday night and Monday. The drinkers on the club tried to forget it but, to this moment, the result is still the same. . .Jets 16; Colts 7 in the most shocking Super Bowl ever played, an unforgettable upset.

It has since been suggested if the Colts had won the way they were supposed to, the Super Bowl would have suffered. The NFL, represented by Green Bay, had romped in the first two Super Bowls and the game might have lost public interest. But the Jets winning as a long shot certainly added credence to the Super Bowl's acceptance. From that aspect, the Colts, if it's any consolation, played a part in enhancing its stature. But they had to lose to do it.

There was deep remorse on the part of the Colts and promises to each other they would live down this terrible thing that happened to them. But they had to wait at least a year before they could get back and, even then, it wasn't to be. They got in trouble at the outset, losing to the Rams and Vikings and winding up with a record of 8 and 5, good only for a second place. Tom Mitchell and Orr were injured and so was Mackey. Any chance the Colts had of going back to the Super Bowl disappeared. The 1969 campaign also found three valuable veterans retiring, Szymanski after 13 years, Brasse with 12 and Boyd with nine.

But coming up for the Colts was their self-made transfer to the realigned American Conference with Pittsburgh and Cleveland. They each were handsomely compensated for the switch. Some fans were angry about the move because the Colts wouldn't be playing the Bears and Packers on a regular basis. But others felt it would be an easier route to the Super Bowl because the competition would be softer. Maybe it would be.

But major things transpired, off the field, that were to change the future of the Colts. Don Klosterman came from the Houston Oilers to be general manager. This meant Hulmes was put in a subordinate position but not for long. He officiated at the Jan. 6 announcement of Klosterman's appointment, which would have been awkward for anyone else, except Hulmes is a kind and gracious individual. But Harry decided shortly thereafter it was time to move on to another job.

The New Orleans Saints hired him as an executive administrator and he was gone. In short order,

To the delight of everyone including the officer with the sunglasses, Jimmy Orr scores another of his many TD's. A winning type of player who was extemely popular with Baltimore fans, Jimmy had a great capacity for getting open and proved to be very durable despite his size. He caught 50 career touchdown passes for the Colts, many of which were gathered in a certain area of the end-zone which was known by everyone as "Orrsville."

Shula also left. He read the hand-writing on the wall and decided the moment was approaching when he could be in jeopardy. Carroll Rosenbloom was on a vacation in the Orient when Shula was contacted by Bill Braucher, a sports writer for *The Miami Herald,* who had been a football teammate when both attended John Carroll University. Braucher wanted to know if Shula would consider coming to Miami. Shula asked Rosenbloom's son, Steve, assistant to the president, if he could have permission to talk with the Dolphins. This was granted. Shula then met with Dolphins' owner Joe Robbie and decided he'd like to become general manager as well as coach. He called Rosenbloom in Hawaii to tell him of his decision and it was made official Feb. 18 that Shula was heading south.

Miami was overjoyed in getting Shula to say "yes" but Rosenbloom charged tampering. Commissioner Pete Rozelle, after conducting an inquiry, decided to award the Colts a 1971 first round draft choice from the Dolphins. This turned out to be Don

McCauley, a strong and dependable halfback from North Carolina. It was a time of turmoil, Rosenbloom and Robbie firing insults; Rozelle pondering what action he should take.

The Colts then were without a coach. Rosenbloom didn't appear to be in any rush to name a replacement. Finally, on April 3, 1970, exactly 44 days after Shula left, the Colts had a new field maestro. It was Don McCafferty, who had been the backfield coach and offensive coordinator under Shula. He was a soft-spoken, patient and quiet man. The players called him the "Easy Rider". He was entirely different from Shula, who was intense, animated and demanding.

So, as the 1970s arrived, things had changed drastically. There was a different general manager, coach and even a new conference. Would it presage success instead of the brutal run of luck they had experienced during the difficult decade that was behind them? Seldom, if ever had any club in NFL history, been dogged by the extreme disappointments, most not of their making, which had frustrated them at all turns for ten straight years.

But 1970, happily, turned it all around. The kicks that were off-line suddenly started to go their way, measurements that came up an inch short were now long enough. It was a year when the Colts learned the breaks of football do eventually even up. The opener in San Diego against the Chargers found rookie Jim O'Brien kicking three field goals, the last one with 56 seconds left, to give the Colts a 16-14 win. This set the tenor of the season, close victories. The Colts didn't look impressive but they were winning and that's what counted.

During the 1960s, they were often awesome but awfully unlucky. It was as if all those past disappointments were going to even-out in one year. The Colts qualified for the Super Bowl, with late rallies and narrow victories marking the season. They won over the Chargers by two points, the Oilers by four, the Packers by three, the Bears by one. It was almost as if it had been pre-ordained this was to be Baltimore's year.

The Super Bowl was different, too. It was the same city, Miami, the Orange Bowl again, but they would be opposing the Dallas Cowboys instead of the Jets.

The Colts decided that what they had done two years before in their Super Bowl approach was going to be entirely different. They were headquartered at Miami Lakes, within a short punt of where Shula, their ex-coach was living. Under the cover of darkness, some of the players visited him for a social call. They didn't want Rosenbloom to know they were still on speaking terms. Instead of the players' wives and children being with the team all week, they were invited to arrive the day before the game and were given rooms at another

hotel. Practice facilities were close by and not 45-minutes away.

Although the Colts had gone to extremes in seeing that their week of practice and preparation leading up to Super Bowl V would in no way be similar to their experience in Super Bowl III, they still played a poor game. The only difference this time was they won, even if it wasn't artistic.

There were eleven turnovers in the zany proceedings. Unitas was intercepted twice and Morrall once. The Colts also fumbled four times. It was far from a classic but few Super Bowls are. There was a feeling of "what's going to happen next?" prevailing because of the bizarre way the game unfolded. At times it was weird. Almost burlesque.

Dallas had two early drives of eight plays each, covering 47 and 57 yards, and each time Mike Clark pumped home field goals, which gave the Cowboys a 6-0 advantage in the second period. But

Arkansas' own Billy Ray Smith puts the clamps on Green Bay halfback Travis Williams. Billy Ray was unquestionably one of the top defensive tackles in Colt history.

129

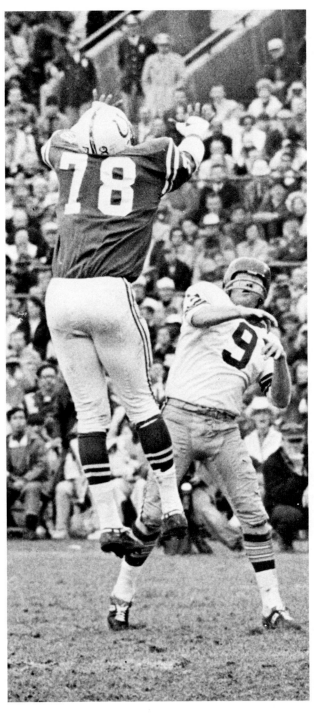

Bubba Smith goes airborne on this pass attempt by the Redskins' Sonny Jurgensen. Bubba played defensive end for five years and made All-Pro in 1970 and 1971.

that was rubbed out by what has to be far and away the most astounding play in Super Bowl history. On third down, Unitas tried to reach Eddie Hinton with a medium deep pass. It was high, Hinton tipped it and then a Cowboy defender, Mel Renfro, got a "finger nail" on the sailing ball. But, instead of being deflected, the pass kept on like it was directed by radar. It wound up in the arms of Mackey at the Cowboy's 45 and he stormed to the end-zone untouched, 75-yards in all, in a freakish happening. It couldn't have been staged that way if you had all day to rehearse. Strictly an accident.

But this was no ordinary game. On O'Brien's try to give the Colts the lead after Mackey's "miracle" TD, the conversion attempt was blocked by Mark Washington and it was 6-6. It was difficult at that moment to visualize an O'Brien place-kick in the last minute deciding the issue. But, meanwhile, other things were happening. Unitas fumbled when he was blasted on a blitz by Lee Roy Jordan and Jethro Pugh recovered at the Colts' 28. Three plays later, Craig Morton fed a seven yard pass to Duane Thomas to make it 13-6 at halftime. What could happen next?

Well, the Colts showed them. Jim Duncan fumbled the kickoff and Dallad recovered. Thomas, trying to reach the goal line, lost control of the ball after he made a "second effort". Duncan redeemed himself by gaining the recovery not before Billy Ray Smith convinced officials the ball belonged to Baltimore. To this day, Dallas players insist they had possession and should have been allowed to retain it. Had the Cowboys scored at that juncture it would have made the count at least 20-6 and changed the entire pattern of play. But Baltimore didn't allow the Cowboys any additional points and got ten themselves, thanks to pass interceptions.

Rick Volk came between a Morton-to-Walt Garrison aerial in the fourth period, returning it 30-yards to the Cowboys' three. Tom Nowatzke, who had been responsible for letting Washington come through to block O'Brien's early conversion try, got the touchdown for the Colts on a two-yard bolt. It was 13-13 and the clock was moving to what many in the crowd of 79,204 felt would go to an overtime decision. But this was a game marked by mistakes as much as it was one of accomplishment. The Cowboys' Morton threw to one of his surest receivers, Dan Reeves. The ball caromed off his hands and, almost as if it was supposed to be, into the grasp of Mike Curtis at the 41. Curtis ran the interception to the 28 and, two plays later, with Morrall holding, O'Brien drilled a 32 yard field goal to win the coveted Super Bowl for Baltimore, 16-13. The Colts' actually jumped for joy.

It was far from smooth and artistic but the Colts didn't care. It was a victory they felt was long owed them. Tackle Bob Vogel expressed his feelings and they were similar to how the entire squad felt. "So what?", he replied, when the luck factor was introduced. "I've had luck decide against us so many times I'm sick of it. I quit being proud years ago when we lost games we should have won. The way I look at it, we're going to get the Super Bowl ring because we won the games that counted this year. We deserve it."

If nothing else, the Colts had followed the "bouncing ball" to the glorious end of the Super Bowl rainbow, meaning a $15,000 check for all players and coaches, and huge horseshoe-designed rings to wear as a constant reminder they were winners of Super Bowl V.

The fans of the Colts were elated, too, but nothing like what happened in 1958 when they battled back to beat the Giants in overtime. But that was an initial championship and, as song writers and poets tell us, nothing ever quite equals the first time.

Don Shula confers with Johnny Unitas and Earl Morrall during workouts prior to Super Bowl III.

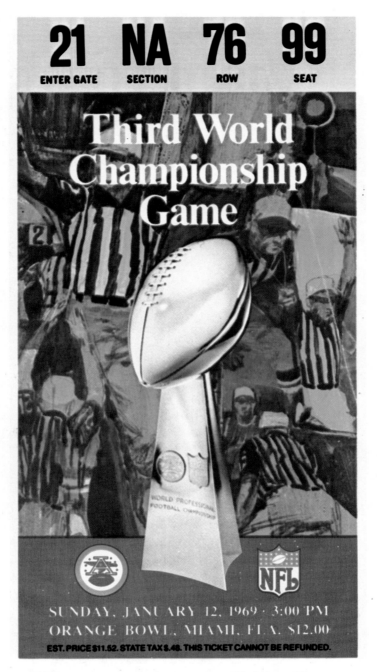

Jets vs Colts

AMERICAN FOOTBALL LEAGUE CHAMPION
NEW YORK JETS VERSUS
NATIONAL FOOTBALL LEAGUE CHAMPION
BALTIMORE COLTS
SUNDAY, JANUARY 12, 1969
ORANGE BOWL, MIAMI, FLORIDA

THIRD WORLD CHAMPIONSHIP GAME/JANUARY 12, 1969, ORANGE BOWL, MIAMI, FLORIDA/PRICE $1.00

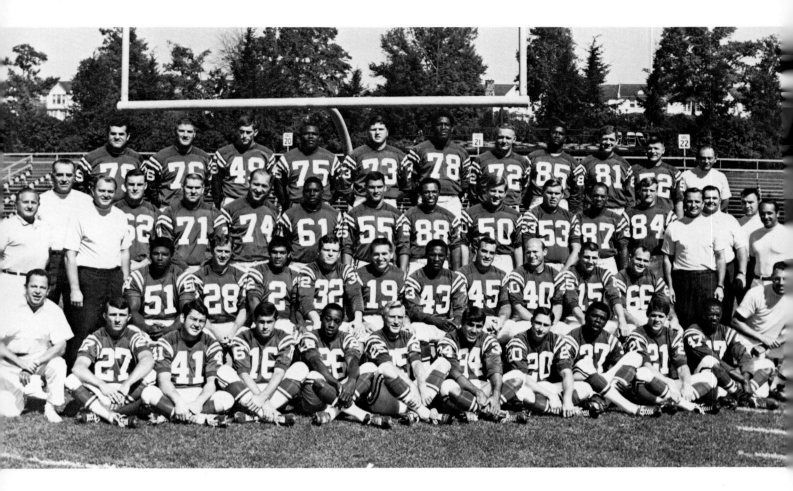

THE 1968 BALTIMORE COLTS

TOP ROW (left to right): (79) Lou Michaels, (76) Fred Miller, (49) David Lee, (75) John Williams, (73) Sam Ball, (78) Bubba Smith, (72) Bob Vogel, (85) Roy Hilton, (81) Ordell Braase, (52) Dick Szymanski, Defensive Line Coach Bill Arnsparger.
SECOND ROW (left to right): Assistant Trainer Dick Spassoff, Offensive Backfield Coach Don McCaffery, Defensive Backfield Coach Chuck Noll, (62) Glenn Ressler, (71) Dan Sullivan, (74) Billy Ray Smith, (61) Cornelius Johnson, (55) Ron Porter, (88) John Mackey, (50) Bill Curry, (53) Dennis Gaubatz, (87) Willie Richardson, (84) Tom Mitchell, Head Coach Dan Shula, Offensive Line Coach John Sandusky, End Coach Dick Bielski, Assistant Trainer John Spassoff.
THIRD ROW (left to right): (51) Bob Grant, (28) Jimmy Orr, (2) Timmy Brown, (32) Mile Curtis, (19) John Unitas, (43) Lenny Lyles, (45) Jerry Hill, (40) Bob Boyd, (15) Earl Morrall, (66) Don Shinnick, Equipment Manager Fred Schubach.
BOTTOM ROW (left to right): Head Trainer Eddie Block, (27) Ray Perkins, (41) Tom Matte, (16) Jim Ward, (26) Preston Pearson, (25) Alex Hawkins, (34) Terry Cole, (20) Jerry Logan, (37) Ocie Austin, (21) Rick Volk, (47) Charlie Stukes.

134

Unitas and Morrall discussing strategy with Don McCafferty during the 1970 championship season.

SUPER BOWL V

Price $1.50

WORLD PROFESSIONAL FOOTBALL CHAMPIONSHIP FOR THE VINCE LOMBARDI TROPHY
Sunday, January 17, 1971 • 2:00 p.m. Orange Bowl, Miami

Baltimore vs Dallas

It was this tackle by George Andrie that put John Unitas out of Super Bowl V with damaged ribs.

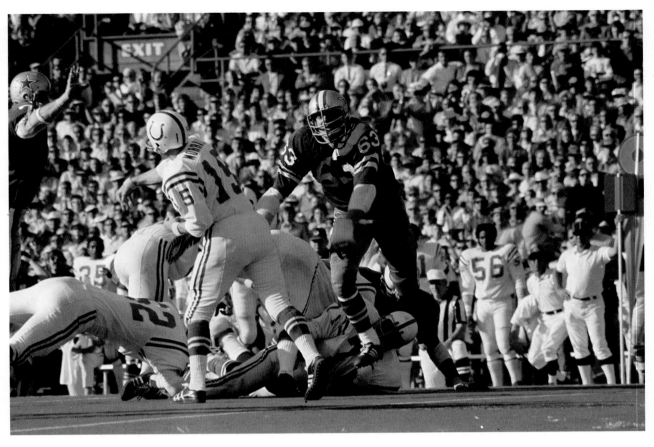

Enter Earl Morrall shown here completing another pass in Super Bowl V, despite a strong rush from the Dallas defenders.

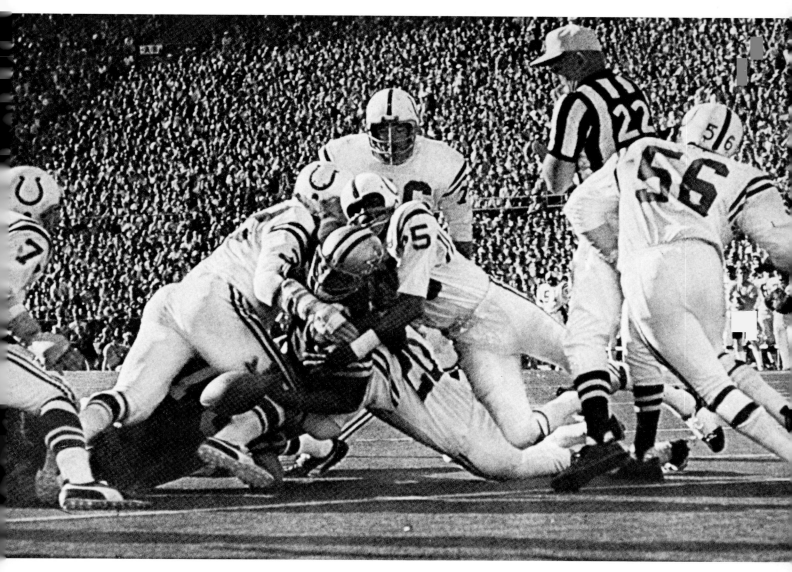

This fumble proved to be very costly for Duane Thomas and the Cowboys. Thomas was giving it the old second-effort when he lost the ball near the end zone and the recovery was awarded to the Colts, still today a highly debatable ruling.

It wasn't Thomas' day. Here a covey of Colt defenders including Roy Hilton, Rick Volk and Jerry Logan stop him for no gain.

*Fred Miller hovers over a fallen Craig Morton in
4th quarter action.*

With only minutes remaining, Dan Reeves bobbled this pass from Craig Morton and the ever-present Mike Curtis intercepted to set up the winning field goal.

The scoreboard sets the stage . . .

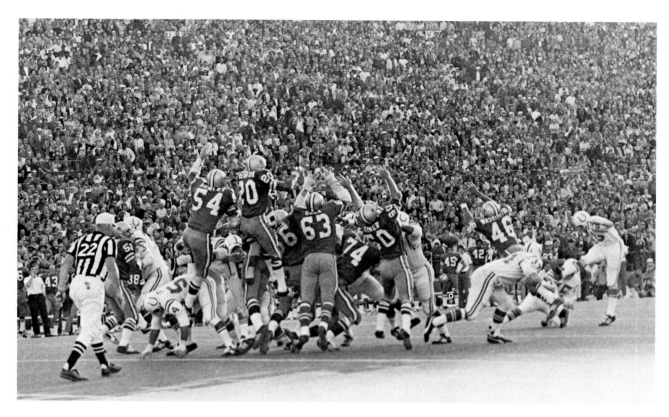

Jim O'Brien kicks (the ball is just above No. 45 of the Cowboys standing on the sidelines)...

Everyone watches...

It's Good!!!

THE 1970 WORLD CHAMPION BALTIMORE COLTS

FIRST ROW *(left to right):* Defensive Line Coach John Sandusky, (48) Larry Conjar, (27) Ray Perkins, (80) Jim O'Brien, (17) Sam Havrilak, (35) Jim Duncan, (23) Jack Maitland, (30) Ron Gardin, (42) Tom Maxwell, (33) Eddie Hinton, (21) Rick Volk, (47) Charlie Stukes, (25) Tom Curtis.

SECOND ROW *(left to right):* Linebacker Coach Hank Bullough, Head Trainer Ed Block, (36) Norm Bulaich, (28) Jimmy Orr, (20) Jerry Logan, (88) John Mackey, (19) John Unitas, (76) Fred Miller, (15) Earl Morrall, (45) Jerry Hill, (87) Roy Jefferson, (41) Tom Matte, Assistant Trainer John Spassoff, Assistant Trainer Dick Spassoff.

THIRD ROW *(left to right):* Offensive Line Coach Lou Rymkus, Head Coach Don McCafferty, (62) Glenn Ressler, (71) Dan Sullivan, (74) Billy Ray Smith, (61) Cornelius Johnson, (51) Bob Grant, (32) Mike Curtis, (50) Bill Curry, (52) Robbie Nichols, (56) Ray May, (84) Tom Mitchell, Defensive Backfield Coach Bob Boyd, Equipment Manager Fred Schubach, End Coach Dick Bielski, Offensive Backfield Coach John Idzik.

FOURTH ROW *(left to right)* (49) David Lee, (75) John Williams, (68) Dennis Nelson, (81) Billy Newsome, (83) Ted Hendricks, (78) Bubba Smith, (65) Jim Bailey, (85) Roy Hilton, (73) Sam Ball, (72) Bob Vogel.

THE 1970 BALTIMORE COLTS

He referred to himself as an "old tin knocker" when he assumed ownership of the Baltimore Colts in 1972 but, in reality, Robert Irsay was a prominent industrialist who gained stature and wealth in the heating and air conditioning business. He bought the Los Angeles Rams for a reported $19 million and then traded the franchise for the Colts.

CHAPTER SEVEN
THE TRADE

What had first brought Baltimore to the attention of potential franchise owners, crowds in excess of 50,000 for exhibition appearances during World War II, became the catalyst for an abrupt change. The public didn't mind buying season tickets, a reported 50,246 for six successive years, plus an announced string of 51 straight sellout regular league games but it had a painful aversion to exhibitions.

It was a fact of life which Rosenbloom, under his administration, hoped to change. In Baltimore's first year in the NFL, 1950, an inflated gathering of only 6,000 came out to see the Colts lose to the 49ers. It was, admittedly, a poor outfit to watch.

But then came 1960, after two world championships, and the most crowd pleasing teams the Colts ever had. They played the Redskins in their lone Baltimore exhibition appearance. The audience count was a modest 6,218. The next year, meeting the Minnesota Vikings at home, featuring a Shaw vs. Unitas matchup, the turnout was 10,208. It was at a time when enthusiasm for the Colts was never higher. Still there was little appeal to come watch them in exhibitions. Kellett, the general manager, surveyed all the empty seats and, while not amused, wise-cracked, "This looks like secret practice".

For the next ten (10) years, the Colts never attempted another home exhibition. But they gave it the "old pro" try...not once but three times in 1971. The fans didn't buy, the Colts and Kansas City Chiefs playing to 16,771; the Colts and Bears to 17,593 and the Colts and Cowboys to 22,291. Obviously, the Baltimore public was not enamored with exhibitions. The Colts had won their first Super Bowl earlier in the year, the cup runneth over with joy but the fans preferred to cool off in Ocean City or to crab at the crabs that weren't biting on their hand lines in Chesapeake Bay. Left to their own option, to accept or reject, they just weren't interested in anything but the real thing. The next season, the Colts headed their pre-season road show to Tampa, which was making noise for an NFL franchise.

Rosenbloom said he was even considering transferring the Colts there. But NFL owners, in an informal survey by this reporter, were opposed to leaving Baltimore. The commissioner, Rozelle, was trying to stay out of the controversy but he, too, promised the Colts weren't going to be uprooted. He was on record with Congress, prior to the NFL merger with the AFL, that none of the existing franchises would be transferred. This was an important reason why approval was granted for the leagues to consolidate. But, apart from legal threats, Rozelle had too much regard for Baltimore to let the Colts depart.

This writer had always voiced the opinion that exhibitions should be played in places like Roanoke, Syracuse, Hershey, Norfolk, Rochester, Portland, Omaha, Louisville and other non-league cities. Rosenbloom claimed we were personally against him but that wasn't true. He used the term "vendetta" and, actually, we had to go to the dictionary to find out what it meant.

Relationships became strained. We were not invited, like other sports writers, to travel with the team. That was his perogative. It was an inconvenience but we made our own arrangements and never missed a kickoff. The team was paramount; it always had been and the owner's attitude to a sports writer was only of minor concern in the overall picture. Suffice to say, some of the things that happened were not any credit to humanity. It was an honest disagreement, a clash of philosophies, and if a man doesn't stand up for what he believes he's not worth much. End of sermon.

Before the exhibition issue came to a boil, the Colts had to get ready to defend their Super Bowl laurels. They had another top season, winning ten, losing four, and finishing second to the surprising 1971 Dolphins, who were 10-3 and 1. The Colts' personnel director, Upton Bell, who had been in the position since the death of Molesworth in 1966, and before that an assistant in the same department for five years, became the general manager of the New England Patriots. He was to put that club on the road to respectability. George Young, who had been a fine tackle at Bucknell and just missed making the 1952 Texans, succeeded Bell in the job. Young had been an assistant in scouting but filled in as offensive line coach in 1970, leading up to the Super Bowl.

An injury to Unitas in the off-season, when he tore an Achilles' tendon playing paddle-ball with Matte at the Towson YMCA, was regarded as a problem but the operation was successful. His leg gave him no bother and he had another good season, even at the advanced football age of 38.

The Colts thumped the Jets, 22-0, in the 1971 seasonal opener. It was a record shattering day for Norm Bulaich, who established a single game Colts' high by rushing for 198 yards on 22 carries. He sprained his ankle in the first quarter but that didn't slow him down. He kept running. The performance rubbed out the mark Ameche put up in his rookie debut of 1955. Bulaich showed speed, poise and an ever-trying attitude that made him easy to like as a player and individual.

Where the Colts, the team, and Shula, the coach, had to deal with the Packers, the team, and Vince Lombardi, the coach, through most of the early 1960s, it became apparent the Dolphins and Shula were going to provide a stern test. Shula had authored a remarkable job of turning around a disorganized Miami team, winning 10 and 4 in his first try, in 1970, plus a playoff chance that failed. There wasn't any doubt the Dolphins were going to be a serious factor in the Eastern Division.

The Colts had lost to the Dolphins in their first 1971 meeting in the Orange Bowl, 17-14, and then got even, 14-3 in Baltimore, a win that resulted in a half-game lead with only one game to play. This meant if the Colts could stay right there for another week and win the final game at home against the Patriots, they would wrap-up the division and be the host for the championship. So another Super Bowl was coming in focus. This all came to sudden revision, however, when the Colts played themselves out of the home field advantage. They lost to the Patriots, 21-17, for what owner Billy Sullivan then called his team's greatest win. Randy Vataha caught an over-the-head pass for 88 yards from Jim Plunkett, his former Stanford battery-mate, that left the crowd of 57,942 at Memorial Stadium reduced to mute silence.

In Cleveland, where the Colts always seemed to be trying to qualify for a championship, they rolled to an impressive 20-3 victory. Don Nottingham, a fire-plug shaped fullback from Kent State, scored both of the Colts' TDs and gained 92 yards. Unitas tossed to Mitchell for 73 yards on five catches in a playoff witnessed by 74,082 at cavernous Municipal Stadium. This put the Colts just one game away from the Super Bowl but it wasn't to be.

The Colts were to face the Dolphins in Miami and decided to go to Florida to get ready, figuring they would get out of the bad Baltimore weather of late December and acclimate themselves to the warm temperatures. They were to workout at the University of South Florida, located in Tampa, and then travel across the Sunshine State to play the Dolphins. The move availed them nothing, except a spirited welcome at the Tampa airport from the fans who had been told they had a chance to get the Colts as permanent residents. The Tampa experience, however, didn't help them. Maybe part of the problem was they had trouble keeping their minds on football with all the attention they were receiving.

The Colts went on to Miami and, playng without injured backs Matte and Bulaich, were shutout, 21-0, the first time it had happened to them since Dec. 13, 1965, or 97 games ago. The Colts were out-hit

Carroll Rosenbloom was the Colt owner from January 11, 1953 to July 26, 1972. . .19 years and three world championships.

but not out-gained, compiling 302 total yards to 286 for the Dolphins. Unitas' passing arm accounted for 224 yards on 20 of 36 completions but a Dick Anderson interception and a determined 62 yard scoring return indicated the intensity the Dolphins had brought with them. They took out the Colts with a wave of awesome blocking and Anderson's tally made it 14-0. Bubba Smith left the field in the late stages complaining of the heat. The Colts had been whipped and it was the Dolphins who were headed to the Super Bowl. So, again, there was disappointment and the Colts blamed themselves for blowing the closing season game to the Patriots, but when you lose it's always easy to find reasons for failure.

The off-season was still filled with talk about transferring to Tampa. Bumper stickers appeared on Maryland cars that read "Don't TAMPA With Our Colts". Plans were disclosed to conduct the next training camp there and the Colts left Westminster for Tampa after 19 years. They also liked the idea of Tampa hosting three exhibitions, or pre-season games, as Bell, the commissioner before Rozelle, liked to call them. But things, meanwhile, were stirring in other directions that were to involve the Colts. Rather team management. There was, of all things, interest being expressed by Rosenbloom in the status of the Los Angeles Rams.

Rosenbloom, who had bought out his Colts' partners in 1964, referred to his situation in Baltimore as "untennable", which was open to debate, but he felt it was time to leave. There had been enormous thrills, satisfaction, recognition and profits. The Rams' franchise, considered the most desirable in all of sports because of its vast drawing power, had become available. Dan Reeves, who had taken the Rams from Cleveland to Los Angeles in 1946, and pioneered the west for major league sports, died in 1971 and his heirs decided to dispose of the club.

There were cursory inquiries, attempts at negotiations and Melvin Durslag, columnist for *The Los Angeles Herald Examiner,* disclosed in 1971, almost a year before it happened, that Rosenbloom might be planning to take over the Rams. Some readers, including other newspapermen, laughed in derision but Durslag had been too good a reporter for too long to believe he would syndicate a column that he took off the wall.

What Durslag predicted actually came to pass. It became a deeply involved transaction and Rosenbloom was credited with quarterbacking a clever coast-to-coast option pass. In effect, he traded the Colts for the Rams and got one of the most desirable properties in sports. Players had been dealt away before but ownerships, franchises and cities had never been swapped. This was unprecedented.

It was a complex arrangement, that may not have happened except for a man named Joe Thomas, who was temporarily out of work, or in a holding pattern over Miami. Thomas, who had been the Colts' line coach in 1954, had quit as chief talent scout of the Dolphins. He had been offered a three year contract with an annual pay hike but was told by Joe Robbie, the owner, he had no chance to ever become the general manager, which was his desire.

So for six months, Thomas stayed in Miami wondering about vacancies elsewhere. He heard about the Rams' franchise being available and of Rosenbloom's interest to go there. Rosenbloom was disenchanted in Baltimore with the aging stadium, the fact the city was reluctant to embrace exhibition games and also with this reporter. There were bitter exchanges between the mayor and other city officials, cooling off periods, dialogue and then more dart-throwing. It made for an unpleasant atmosphere.

There were threats to pull out of Baltimore and build a stadium in Columbia or Baltimore County. But bold, out-spoken Dale Anderson, chief executive of Baltimore County, said, "The Colts belong to Baltimore. They are important to the city. We don't want them because they are Baltimore's property and always have been. I love to go to Memorial Stadium to watch them play."

When Don McCafferty was fired five games into the 1972 season, offensive line coach John Sandusky took over the reins until the end of the season, posting a respectable 4-5 record.

There was even a facietious story written referring to them as the Sparrows Point Colts or the Parkville Colts or the Cockeysville Colts.

Thomas knew abut the controversy ensuing in Baltimore and also had read that Rosenbloom was keen to land the Rams. He decided he would call Commissioner Rozelle to ask if he put together a group of buyers could he get involved in the Rams' sales talks. The answer was yes. Thomas' doctor, the man who operated on him for open heart surgery, told him that his brother, attorney George Elias, might help him find some rich investors.

This led to Robert Irsay, an air conditioning-heating magnate who lived in Winnetka, Ill., and also in Bal Harbour, Fla. Another possible investor was W.H. (Bud) Keland, of Racine, Wis., who had once been a minority stockholder of the Dolphins. But Keland backed away at the last minute and, as Irsay, said later, "I ate the whole thing".

The way the announcement was made, Irsay bought the Rams from the Reeves' estate for $19 million and then traded those holdings to Rosenbloom for the Colts. But there were other considerations, extra financial inducements, which Rosenbloom gave that made Irsay happy. Thomas, in turn, became the general manager and went off to join the Colts in their training camp at Tampa.

Thomas never formally introduced himself to the

149

In two and a half years, Don McCafferty ("Easy Rider") posted a 20-10-1 regular season record and was 4-1 in the playoffs, including a Super Bowl title in 1970. Here he's being hoisted aloft by Roy Hilton and John Mackey after the Colts defeated the Oakland Raiders 27-17 to win the AFC championship game in 1970.

squad that first summer. He was asked why not and explained the important thing is, "I know your jersey numbers", which is really what football is all about. Tampa still had designs on attracting the Colts but Thomas quickly said there was no chance of that happening and, besides, they wouldn't be back for training camp either but would settle somewhere close to Baltimore for pre-season drills in the future.

" I was there watching and I didn't like what I saw," said Thomas. "I didn't see much discipline and the team was getting old. I figured I would wait to see how the season went and then make some moves for the next year."

But, as Baltimore was to find out, Thomas might think he is going to be patient but that's not his style. Five games and four losses into the season, Thomas started to make moves. He told coach Don McCafferty, without warning, he was fired.

The Colts were grumbling. They said Thomas was destroying the team but the new general manager insisted most of the players were old and needed to be replaced. When he got rid of McCafferty, he announced John Sandusky, the line coach, would finish out the year. Irsay later said, after an exciting 20-19 win over the Cincinnati Bengals, that

Howard Shnellenberger was the quiet and reserved head coach for the 1973 season and three games of the 1974 campaign before general manager Joe Thomas was told to take over the field responsibilities.

Sandusky would be retained for 1973. But Thomas said, less than a minute later, "Don't write it unless you want it to look bad, because Sandusky isn't going to be the coach. I'm telling you that as strongly as I can make it."

The season was in frequent turmoil. Two players, one retired and one active, said we were writing too many complimentary things about Thomas. We told them if we needed their imput, we'd ask, but preferred to form our own opinions. Late in the season, it was apparent Unitas, if he had thoughts of continuing to play, was going to have to find another city and he requested a deal. Earlier, Thomas had called him at the locker room and said he was telling the coach to play Marty Domres.

Thomas and Irsay talked with the San Diego Chargers and sold Unitas' contract outright for $150,000. Prior to the move, this reporter met with Thomas and then publicity director Ernie Accorsi in a meeting at Charles Street restaurant to try to convince the general manager that Unitas should be retained because of his immense contributions to the team and his popularity. We said to Thomas, "America doesn't have many heroes left. You can't put Unitas on waivers." Thomas wasn't impressed, merely answering, "Why not, he was there before, wasn't he?" It sounded impersonel and demeaning but it wasn't. It was just Joe's way. We next told him, in the same conversation, to consider what Unitas had done for football. "I don't look at it that way," he replied, "Look what football had done for Unitas. The game is always more important than the player."

Along with sending Unitas to San Diego, it appeared that Thomas was conducting a dispersal sale. He was dealing fast and furiously, sending veterans to points near and far and asking, for the most part, only the right to stockpile draft choices. His prediction that Sandusky wouldn't be retained was right, too. He released the entire coaching staff and said all were free to shop elsewhere.

Thomas, meanwhile, decided on Howard Schnellenberger, the offensive coordinator of the Dolphins, as the Colts' new head coach. It is Thomas' opinion, than and now, that coaches aren't important. "It's like a cabinetmaker working with wood", he analogized. "Give him a piece of maple and he'll make a good piece of furniture. But let him have cotton wood to work with and it won't look like much and it won't last. Players make coaches."

There was surprise when the 1973 draft came on and Thomas went for Bert Jones on the first round, after grabbing off the New Orleans Saints' first choice, and keeping his own to pick Joe Ehrmann. Both were to make the grade and provide help for the future. The Colts were building, Thomas said, but the public didn't understand and Unitas'

Joe Thomas came to the Colts in 1972 as general manager but was first associated with the team in 1954 as a coach. During the interim, he had a prominent hand in building Super Bowl teams with the Miami Dolphins and the Minnesota Vikings. He is recognized as an excellent evaluator of playing talent and as a smart trader, as witness his frequent wheeling and dealing during his five years in Baltimore.

multitude of friends took exception to what Thomas had done to Baltimore's all-time favorite. McCafferty, meanwhile, was signed by the Detroit Lions to be their head coach.

Going into his first full year, Thomas, in 1973, had utilized the off-season for what seemed a string of un-ending moves. Unitas was sold on Jan. 22 to San Diego and Matte was sent to the same team two days later for an eighth round choice, who turned out to be Ray Oldham. Then he grabbed center Fred Hoaglin from the Browns for the Chiefs' third pick that he earlier obtained for Eldridge Dickey. It was Joe wheelin' and dealin' and the fur was flying.

Bill Curry was sent to Houston for the Oilers' third round choice, which Thomas turned into Bill Olds. Billy Newsome and a fourth round selection had gone to New Orleans for a first round pick that was transformed into Bert Jones. Bulaich was dealt to Philadelphia for a fourth round in 1973 and a second round draft right in 1974. Those three transactions all came about on Jan. 29, 1973. Things were happening so fast you wondered if Thomas could keep straight in his own mind, what he had and didn't have.

Danny Sullivan, Fred Miller, Tom Nowatzke, Jim O'Brien, Charles Stukes and Jerry Logan also were sent elsewhere, usually for draft choices. Thomas gave up a third round to land Guard Elmer Collett

152

prior to training camp and then, on the day the camp workouts started, July 16, he unloaded Bubba Smith to the Oakland Raiders for Raymond Chester.

There was little question Thomas was calling the shots. There came a time when he was unhappy with Schnellenberger playing Nottingham. He wanted to see Lydell Mitchell get more activity. So Thomas settled the situation by taking it upon himself to deal Nottingham and a sixth round draft choice to the Dolphins for Hubert Ginn. "I'd like to see them use Nottingham now," said Thomas.

That was the way it continued. Thomas was moving players all over the league. But he accomplished what he was after . . .youth instead of age. It didn't mean the promising rookies were going to be better than the departing proven veterans but Thomas insisted the Colts were on their way back as a contender.

His critics claimed he was trying to make the Colts to his own shape and design and that he resented the earlier success of the club. Wrong. "It's not ego," he said. "It's pride. And if you don't have a desire to do the best job every day, regardless of what it is you're doing, then you aren't any good to yourself. I could go around to all the cocktail parties, slap everybody on the back, give them a lot of baloney and they'd all be saying what a good guy Joe Thomas is. But I'm not a politician."

Thomas, even though he made daring moves, was sensitive to criticism. This made him something of a paradox. But there was no question he had helped build two other teams that had gone on to the Super Bowl, the Vikings and Dolphins, but he didn't believe the coaching supplied by Bud Grant and Shula had as much to do with the success as the players he had drafted, traded for and left them, after he moved on to other pursuits.

The Colts, in the throes of being dismantled and put back together again by Thomas, flattened out to a 4-10 showing under Schnellenberger, who wasn't too unlike McCafferty in personality. Jones had played more than most rookie quarterbacks and wasn't overly impressive. It was obvious Schnellenberger preferred to let Domres play and bring Jones along. But the 1974 schedule was only two and a half games old when the lid blew. Another explosion.

Irsay had asked Schnellenberger, while the Colts were being ripped apart by the Philadelphia Eagles, to take out Domres and put in Jones. According to Irsay, he didn't like the kind of language Schnellenberger used in his reply. So he fired him. Irsay personally went in the locker room to tell the players Schnellenberger had been dropped and Thomas would take over. It was a difficult place for Thomas but he was there, whether he wanted to be or not.

QTR	BUF	BAL	BALL ON	DOWN	TO GO	BUF	T.O. LEFT	BAL	TIME
4	0	28	37	3	6	3		3	5:23

*A very happy/sad occasion. This was John Unitas'
last TD pass as a Colt. The date: December 3,
1972; the receiver: Eddie Hinton. The end of an era.*

He was doing what Driskill had been told to do in
1948, be both the coach and general manager, and,
again, like it was with Driskill, the dual role was not
of his choosing. The Colts went through another
poor year but, actually, the team looked better than
its 2-12 record indicated. There was recognizable
improvement among the young players and it
seemed to be only a question of time until they
gained maturity and found out they could win.

But the Colts needed a coach. Thomas offered
Irsay the idea of Hank Stram, who had led Kansas
City to Super Bowl IV, but the owner wasn't
impressed. The other possibility was Ted
Marchibroda, who had been an assistant for 14 years
with the Redskins, Rams and then back to the
Redskins. He also had been one of the quarterbacks
the Steelers retained when Unitas had been let go
as a rookie in 1955.

It's Thomas' recollection that when he talked with
Marchibroda he told him that he, Thomas, would
be making the decisions on personnel. But
Marchibroda insists that aspect wasn't discussed.
Whether it was or not, it was a diffrence that led to
problems a year later and the kind of fireworks you
don't get to see on the Fourth of July.

153

Bert Jones . . . the beginning of a new era.

CHAPTER EIGHT
TRIUMPHANT TURN

When Ted Marchibroda became the eleventh head coach of the Colts since the franchise was born in 1947, there was general sympathy expressed in his behalf. It was believed the strong-willed Thomas would over-power him and, once more, another change would have to be made. Thomas had not shown any tolerence with coaches. He had, for the record, gone through Don McCafferty, John Sandusky, Howard Schnellenberger and even himself in three years. But the actual Schnellenberger firing, in the box-score, was attributed to Irsay; not Thomas.

It's not generally known but Joe had even considered continuing as coach for 1975 but Irsay discouraged the idea. So Thomas went for Marchibroda, after giving some thought to Paul Wiggins and Stram. At the press conference announcing Marchibroda's appointment, Thomas, to a question, made it emphatic he was running the show. It was a blunt statement. Maybe Marchibroda didn't hear him but Thomas said it for everyone else in the room to understand.

Certainly, Marchibroda at that time didn't offer rebuttal or challenge. He was obviously pleased to get the opportunity to move up after laboring in the vineyards for 14 years. "They say coaches don't want to work for Joe Thomas," said Joe Thomas, "but so many men have been calling me for this job I practically had to disconnect my phone and hide out in the woods."

Marchibroda was quiet-spoken and described by Bill McPeak, who had given him his first coaching job in 1961 with the Redskins, "as reminding you of an altar boy". His habits were exemplary, meaning he didn't smoke, drink or tell blue stories. Art Rooney, whose Pittsburgh Steelers had made Marchibroda their first round draft choice in 1953 from St. Bonaventure, said, "If they can't play for Ted they can't play for anybody."

The man was endowed with patience and, obviously, had a way with quarterbacks. He had played the position himself and later worked with devising offensive game plans for George Allen, when he coached for him in Los Angeles and Washington. In the spring of 1975, Marchibroda had quarterbacks Jones and Domres meet with him for indoctrination sessions. They covered basics, recognizing defense and how best to attack them. When camp started, it meant Marchibroda and his signal-callers were on the same page, knew what to do and how to go about getting it done.

The Colts won only two of six outings in the exhibition season and had a difficult early schedule, having to face three playoff teams of the previous year, the Raiders, Rams and Bills, after opening on the road against the Chicago Bears. The players, as close as they are to coaches, frankly didn't know if Marchibroda was going to be able to lead them out of the wilderness. They were non-commital about him. But the afternoon before the NFL opener, we met up with an assistant coach, Frank Lauterbur, in the lobby of the Water Tower Hyatt House in Chicago, where the team was staying. "I believe we're going to be able to turn this thing around," said Lauterbur. "I have a lot of confidence in Ted. He can coach and I feel the players will want to win for him."

The next day, the Colts made an impressive start under Marchibroda, beating the Bears, 35-7, and more than doubling the yardage totals. For the next three weeks, against clubs which had been in the playoffs the year before, it was anticipated the Colts would be wiped off the field. But it didn't happen. They lost 31-20 to the Raiders; to the Rams, 24-13, and the Bills, 38-31, plus another defeat by the Patriots, 21-10. All were respectable showings. Baltimore had led in all four games and these were the last ones they were to lose because the Colts quickly reversed themselves and reeled off victories the rest of the way, nine in all, only two short of the club record Shula's 1964 outfit had registered.

All over the NFL the talk was about the amazing Baltimore turn-around. There had actually never been anything comparable to it in the history of the league. The Colts had been 2 and 12, dead-last the previous season, but were now 10 and 4. It was so remarkable Marchibroda was unanimously voted "Coach of the Year" and Thomas "Executive of the Year", two honors which left no room for challenge.

One of the highlights of the surprising showing was what happened in Orchard Park, N.Y., playing the Bills and losing, 21-0, after O.J. Simpson had zipped 44-yards on a run and caught scoring passes of 22 and 32 yards from Joe Ferguson. Lydell Mitchell took a nine-yard pass from Jones to get the Colts on the scoreboard but the Bills snapped back on their next possession, Bob Chandler scoring on a toss from Ferguson to make it 28-7. Time was running out in the second period when the Colts moved to the 15-yard line. The obvious thought was to go for the field goal and cut the lead. But the Colts faked the kick and Domres lobbed softly to Bill Olds for a touchdown. Less than a minute later, after a Buffalo punt, Jones "went for the works" and threw long downfield to Roger Carr, who came under the ball and took it across the goal line on a spectacular

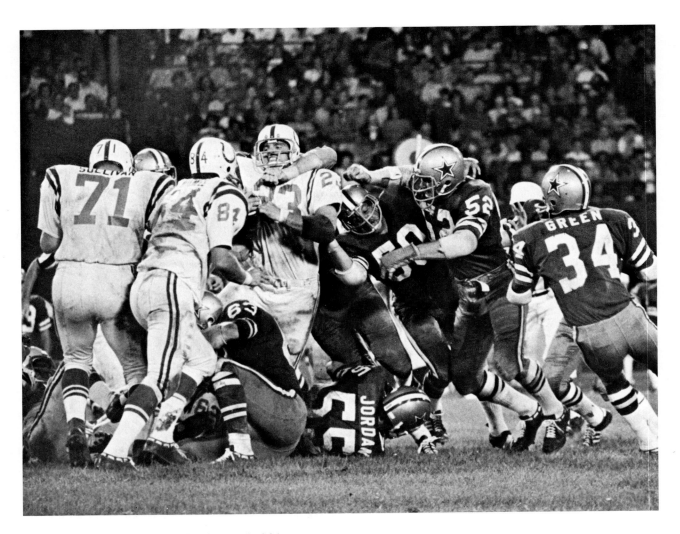

Eight year veteran Don McCauley traded his "Carolina Blue" for the "Colts Blue" when he was drafted number one in 1971. He's been a starter at both halfback and fullback for the Colts and has led the team in rushing TD's for the last two seasons. Last year he caught 51 passes, tops on the club.

89-yard scoring play. The Bills were shocked at the way the Colts had retaliated.

The Colts went on to get three more scores in the second half, all in the fourth period, as Mitchell ran for 11 and 12 yards and Jones carried for 19. This meant the Colts, after trailing 21-0, had erupted for five straight touchdowns in a 42-35 conquest before the largest crowd, 77,320, that would see them all year.

There were two wins over the Dolphins counted in the streak of nine in a row, the first being a 33-17 win in the Orange Bowl when Domres took over for the injured Jones in the second quarter and directed a run-oriented offense to a 31-point splurge. Bruce Laird had tackled Benny Malone for an early saftey. The Dolphins, however, lost Bob Griese, their quarterback, to an injury and he was out the rest of the year. The "new" Colts were impressive and the win added much to their confidence. They were immensely pleased when 10,000 fans, almost like the good ole days, turned out to welcome them home at Friendship Airport.

One of the most memorable contests in the Colts' history took place Dec. 14 in Memorial Stadium. The Colts trailed the Dolphins by a full game in the standings and at the end of three quarters were behind, 7-0. They faced up to the situation and took the ball 86-yards on an impressive drive as tackle George Kunz escorted Mitchell over the goal line from six yards out to tie the score. That's how it was at the end of regualtion time. Now Baltimore was to see its first sudden-death game in Memorial Stadium. The Dolphins won the toss, just as the Giants had in 1958 in Yankee Stadium. They moved to mid-field and punted. It was Larry Seiple who kicked the ball out of bounds at the Colts' four yard line after only 2:15 had been played in the extra period. Now it was the Colts' turn to try. And it was an impressive push upfield after being backed against their own goal line. They maintained possession for 17 plays, numbering 12 runs and 4 passes, plus one sack, to advance to the Dolphins' 14 yard line. With 59,398 fans, an honest count, creating a din that was more like the sounds emanating from a bubbling volcano, Domres knelt on one knee, caught the snap, placed the ball and Toni Linhart made the winning field goal good from 31 yards away. It was a 10-7 triumph and put the Colts in a tie with the Dolphins.

After the game, disappointed but gracious, Shula said, "I give the Colts all the credit in the world. Seiple knocked the ball out on their four yard line and you wouldn't want to be in much better position than that. The Colts were in a hole but came out of it. And their kicker, Linhart, took the pressure and made the field goal. It hurts for us to lose that way but the Colts earned it."

The next Sunday, the Colts clinched their division,

the first time since 1970, with a 34-21 win over the Patriots. Thomas was unhappy in the press box most of the game when he said the Colts didn't have what to him indicated the kind of attitude a team should have when it was going for a title. The Dolphins had the same record as the Colts, 10-4, but the tiebreaker was determined by the fact the Colts had beaten them in head-to-head competition. So it was on to Pittsburgh to engage the Steelers, defending Super Bowl champions, in the playoff elimination.

On a cold afternoon in Three Rivers Stadium, the Colts had to go most of the way without Jones. He went to the sidelines early with a bruised muscle in his throwing arm and Domres came on to sub. The Colts used a Lloyd Mumphord interception that paved the way for a Domres-to-Glenn Doughty touchdown pass and a Nelson Munsey fumble recovery that led to a field goal by Linhart for a 10-7 advantage midway in the third period. A Domres' interception was returned to the seven yard line by Mel Blunt and then Rocky Bleier put Pittsburgh on top, 14-10. A Bradshaw score, on a two yard run, made it 21-10 and the game was apparently out-of-reach. But Jones forgot his arm miseries and, after warming-up, re-entered the game to take the Colts to the three-yard line. Linebacker Jack Ham shot the gap and blasted Jones with a violent tackle. The ball rolled free and Andy Russell retrieved it and ran 93 yards for the final touchdown making the score 28-10.

Domres felt he had lost the game by not being able to get the job done after Jones was hurt. But this was folly. "I belive I could have done a lot better if I had some time in practice working with the first unit during the week," he said later. Marchibroda, knowing how a quarterback felt after a losing effort, tried to console Marty and sat with him on the team bus as the Colts made their way to the airport. The Steelers, meanwhile, went rollicking on to their second straight Super Bowl triumph.

Even though the Colts lost to the Steelers, their season was an immense success, emphasized by the fact no club had ever been 2-12 one year and 10-4 the next. It was said by some observers that Thomas resented the acclaim that was heaped on Marchibroda. But he came close to getting equal treatment when the post-season laurels were handed out. The Thomas' drafts had been productive, bringing such talented young players as Jones, Ehrmann, Carr, Mike Barnes, David Taylor, Ray Oldham, John Dutton, Fred Cook, Ken Huff, Marshall Johnson and Roosevelt Leaks.

Would the Colts be able to keep functioning on a winning note or were they to be regarded as pretender instead of a contender? That was the next question. The exhibition season of 1976 commenced with wins over the Browns and

The Bears' Wayne Moss pretty much tells the story here. Thats Fred Miller (76), Bubba Smith (78) and Roy Hilton sacking Bear quarterback Bobby Douglas during a 1971 exhibition game won by the Colts, 21-13.

Redskins but then they dropped four in a row and looked progressively worse doing it. The last exhibition was in Pontiac Stadium with the Lions and it was a game when both clubs, getting ready for the regular season, wanted to bring everything together. It didn't happen. The Colts not only lost 24-9 but played with little enthusiasm. They were as flat as they had ever been. A bad, bad exhibition.

When the sports writers reached the locker room, the door was shut for longer than is normally expected. The word was passed that Ehrmann had collapsed from heat prostration and was suffering from hyper-ventilation. He was being treated by the team doctor and trainers Eddie Block and Mike O'Shea. Finally, an ambulance crew was summoned and Ehrmann, gasping for breath, was wheeled out and taken to the hospital. Coach Rick Forzano of the Lions stopped by to inquire of Ehrmann's condition. He was worried and offered his help.

Then the dressing room door opened again and Irsay came out. He was accompanied by friends he had brought to the game. Reporter Richard Kucner of *The News American* had been close to the locker room entrance and said, "Some kind of a fight was going on in there". It wasn't anything physical, as it turned out, but it was Irsay telling the team how sorry it had played and he was threatening to fire the coach or bring him some new assistants. Some players screamed, "No, no don't do that".

Jones, when questioned about what transpired behind closed doors, said, "We've been through a traumatic experience and would appreciate it if you reporters didn't ask us questions about what went on." Most of the Colts were dazed. They knew they had played a poor game, they were worried about Ehrmann's condition and were stunned over the Irsay oratory. Marchibroda decided he couldn't operate with those kind of interruptions. He also felt Thomas was becoming too strong a force, telling him what to do and he resented that. But he didn't honestly know how to handle it.

Marchibroda told friends he was going to ask advice of this reporter, who had been close to the Colts' scene for most of the team's existence, or else talk with another man. He took the other option and was advised to put his cards on the table with Irsay. A meeting was held two days later at the Milwaukee Yacht Club, where Irsay had his 60-foot boat, the "Mighty-I", docked. The session went on for the better part of six hours. Irsay told Marchibroda that Thomas was in charge of the team, the one who would continue to make decisions, but he was hopeful Ted would stay, But Marchibroda said he couldn't live with that kind of a situation. He decided to quit. They tried to get him to reconsider but he held firm. So the announcement was made that Marchibroda had resigned and now Thomas and Irsay were looked upon as villains by most of the press and public.

The players spoke out in support of their coach. Jones called for the fans to stay home from the games, a boycott. He said, "If you have a pile of lumber on a corner lot, you need a builder to create a house and that's what Marchibroda has done for us. We back him 100 percent." Jones credited Marchibroda with his own improvement and took the role of team spokesman.

If Marchibroda was leaving then so were three of his assistants, Maxie Baughan, George Boutselis and Whitey Dovell. This left Frank Lauterbur, Pete McCulley and Jerry Smith. In an effort to close the ranks, Thomas offered the job to Baughan but he said he wasn't interested. Baughan then amended his position. He said he would accept if he could be paid a certain figure, totally exhorbitant, which Thomas laughed at.

Commissioner Pete Rozelle was then apprised of the situation unfolding in Baltimore. It's not his place to get involved in club disputes but he went far enough to say he was ready to help mend the breach. It was for the overall good of the league, Rozelle had been told, if he could restore order. He was calm in his approach and quietly assisted in bringing about a solution. Mayor William Donald Schaefer even paid the Colts a visit and told Tomas he would do whatever he wanted. The mayor also pointed a finger at Jones and said, "I didn't like you telling fans not to come to the games."

It was apparent the Colts were going to have to get Marchibroda to return if they were to have any kind of a season. But Thomas said, "He walked out so let him keep walking." The players were firmly aligned with the coach and demanding his return. Thomas didn't like it but, under extreme pressure, had to bring Marchibroda back as head coach and agree to let him be in charge of all decisions relative to player personnel. It was the beginning of the end for Thomas, although at the time he still appeared to be in control and had Irsay's support. When Irsay was later asked what points Marchibroda objected to in his showdown meeting in Milwaukee, he said, "Oh, just a bunch of mini-stuff".

The Colt players had put themselves in a corner by aligning with their coach and the blistering heat they had applied to Irsay and Thomas. What would happen? The answer came quickly, in the opening game, the Colts going to Schaefer Stadium in Foxboro, Mass., where Jones took matters in hand with an exceptional performance, completing 17 of 23 passes for 190 yards, including two touchdown tosses to Glenn Doughty. Lydell Mitchell ran for 73 yards and got 72 more on six receptions. "We felt like somebody had pulled a weight off our chest when we won," said veteran Jim Cheyunski. "The pressure was really on us to win." And they did, 27-13.

It was to be a year when the Colts turned all the

adversity and aggravation into a plus. They also strengthened Marchibroda's position and at season's end it was Thomas who unexpectedly got fired, not the coach. This came after Marchibroda had won more games than the year before, eleven, was popular with the team and Thomas over-played his hand with Irsay. Early in the season, Thomas talked with Irsay about the extension of his contract and was offered a sizeable raise but he didn't think it was enough. He told Irsay he would prefer to defer talk about it until the end of the year, citing the fact his wife, Judi, had been in an auto accident and he was too worried to go into details of what was to be his new financial deal.

"I never had 20 seconds worth of trouble with Bob Irsay," was the claim put forth later by Thomas. There also was an occasion when Thomas asked Irsay if he could have permission to talk with Rankin Smith, owner of the Atlanta Falcons, about taking a

Norm Bulaich barrels through a gaping hole, compliments of center Bill Curry (50) and John Mackey. Norm's best day as a Colt came on Sept. 19, 1971 when he rushed for 198 yards against the Jets, a club record.

job there. Irsay agreed. Thomas returned from Atlanta saying he had been offered a chance to buy into ownership and Smith was even going to help finance the deal. Smith also drove Thomas around the Atlanta suburbs during his visit and told him the more desirable places to live. But that was as far as they got.

Irsay, meanwhile, was saying he wanted to keep both Thomas and Marchibroda. He had Jones come to his office in Skokie, Ill., and fill him in on how the players felt. The team had a record of 11 and 3, a game better than the season before, as Mitchell ran for 1,200 yards and broke his own record set only the previous year. Carr averaged 25.9 yards with every catch, the best ever by a Colt, and scored eleven touchdowns. Jones missed by a fraction of beating out the Raiders' Ken Stabler for the passing title but was voted the "most valuable player" in the league by a vote of the players. Mitchell, Carr,

Bruce Laird puts his best foot backward, right into the face of an unidentified New York Jet. A seven year veteran at safety, Bruce is one of the surest tacklers in the league and holds a number of Colt records for kickoffs.

Toni Linhart is closing in fast on just about every Colt field goal record. He has a career field goal percentage of 64.8, a club record.

Jones, Dutton, Kunz and Linhart made the Pro Bowl squad, the most representation since the Colts won the Super Bowl in 1971.

As for the post-season activity the Colts made it to the first play-off with the Steelers but, again, went under. It was embarrassing. . . 40-14, as the Steelers rolled to 526 yards to only 170 by the Colts. The game was such a runaway that the crowd of 60,020 started to leave early, which, as it turned out, may have averted an immense human tragedy. A small air plane crashed in the top deck of the end-zone after earlier making a pass near the scoreboard at the opposite end of Memorial Stadium. This reporter and David Ailes, sports editor from *The Greensboro, (Pa.) Tribune-Review,* were the closest to the plane as it came in and almost landed at the 50-yard line, on an approach from the north, through the open-end of the stadium. It suddenly ascended at a sharp angle, passed over both of us as it banked to the left and crashed in the empty stands. There was no loss of life and the pilot, Donald Kreiner, suffered only minor injuries.

Had the game not been a rout, some of the fans would have still been in their seats and there's no telling how many casualties may have resulted from the accident. The picture of a plane rammed in the upper deck of the Stadium made page one in most newspapers in the country, even around the world. It just wasn't the way a football season normally comes to an end. The Colts played poorly and Marchibroda said it was apparent to him they needed more quality players, a statement Thomas interpreted as an attempt by the coach to put the blame on him. But, so far as the public was concerned, its attention was diverted from the dismal Colts' showing to the plane crash.

Now the angle, regarding the organization, was what solution would be made to repair the Thomas-Marchibroda break? It was to be a startling windup. At the beginning of the schedule, it was Marchibroda quitting but a month and a day after the season ended, when both the Colts and the plane had come crashing in Memorial Stadium, it was Thomas who was swept out of his office. Two of Irsay's attorneys confronted him after he returned from a luncheon honoring Jones and Kunz and served notice his services were no longer desired. "It hit me like a death in the family," said Thomas late that night. "I never had any trouble with Bob Irsay. But the 'little altar boy' caused the problem."

The year had been filled with continuing controversy, including the stormy scene following the final exhibition, the resignation of Marchibroda and the after-season firing of Thomas. Our personal opinion to this day is Marchibroda was wrong in backing the owner in a corner and Thomas errored in forgetting Irsay owned the team. Joe also was negotiating his contract with the kind of tactics you

And speaking of records, here's the dean of the Colts (13 years), David Lee, who holds just about every punting record on the club.

163

usually expect from a player, not a club executive. Irsay figured at that interval Marchibroda was more essential to the Colts' immediate future, which made Thomas expendable. Irsay, pure and simple, put his priorities with the coach.

It was an upheaval that was distressing, brought on by the strong passions, emotions and egos that come into play in situations like this. The Colts now had vacancies to fill in their administration and Irsay was ready. He turned to Dick Szymanski, the club's director of pro personnel, to be the new general manager and executive vice-president. And Szymanski brought in Ernie Accorsi, who had been the team's public relations director before going to the league office as Assistant to the President of the National Football Conference. Accorsi enjoyed his work with the league but missed the competitive feeling that comes with being identified with a particular team.

Szymanski's duties were limited to negotiating player contracts and handling other administrative functions. Marchibroda was to have final say on all player drafts, trades and acquisitions. It was obvious from the outset that Marchibroda, Szymanski and Accorsi were going to try to function in harmony. The turmoil had subsided and the situation was tranquil.

Marchibroda gained much of the strength that had previously belonged to Thomas but overall responsibilities were more divided between the coach, Szymanski and Accorsi. The changes were well-received by the public, especially the anti-Thomas faction, but there was no way to deny he had asembled the parts for continuing respectability and title challenges. It was Thomas' belief Szymanski and Accorsi had 'done him in' but this wasn't the case at all. Both had been strong defenders of his actions when they worked for him and didn't enter into a plot to have him overthrown. They were loyal.

The Colts in 1977 continued their winning ways with the newly arranged leadership. Most of the attention was directed to the field instead of the front office, which was refreshing. The team figured most of its competition in the Eastern Division would come from the Patriots and the assumption was true. But the Dolphins also were to be a factor. The three clubs went to the final week of play and it was still undetermined which one was going to win. A freak development took place when the Colts got beat by the Lions, 13-10, in an upset and the loss all but eliminated the chances of the Patriots, who had just knocked off the Dolphins, 14-10. It was an odd quirk in the playoff system that was used to break ties. The Colts actually profited by losing to the Lions, even though it was the poorest performance yet given by a Marchibroda team.

A fumble by Jones the next week in the Patriots'

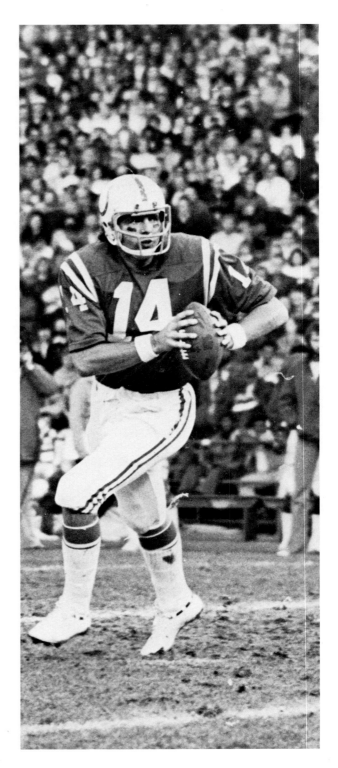

Marty Domres came to the Colts in a 1972 trade from Houston and was asked to play a very difficult role, that of filling in the spot vacated by John Unitas. Highly regarded personally, it was a tough act to follow.

In his three years as head coach, Ted Marchibroda has lead the Colts to first place in the Eastern Division of the AFC each year, posting an overall regular season record of 31—11—0.

game in Baltimore appeared to be recovered by Sam Hunt but referee Frank Silva said he had blown his whistle before the ball came rolling free. The Colts scored soon thereafter, held on to win, 30-24, and had themselves their third Eastern Division championship. But, again, they weren't able to survive the first round of the playoffs. That's what the critics reminded them and they're right so far as the record goes but there's more to it than that.

The Colts gave a far better performance against the Raiders, the defending Super Bowl champions, than they had been able to do against the Steelers the two previous years. In fact, it became a game that rates with the finest they ever played, even if they had to lose it in overtime — specifically double

overtime. It was a 31-31 score at the end of regulation, thanks to Errol Mann driving home a 22-yard field goal with only 26 seconds left on the clock. The Raiders swept 58 yards in the drive and if Mann misses, with fourth down and a foot to go, it's all over and the Colts win. "It's easy to go for it", said coach John Madden later. "The hard thing is to send the field goal team out there but I didn't have any doubt that being the right decision."

Then came the "Russian Roulette" aspects of overtime. The first team to score wins and remains alive in the Super Bowl count-down; the loser waits until next year. Mike Barnes blocked another Mann FG try from the Colts' 48 and that prolonged the pulsating issue. In their first overtime possession, the Colts moved to third-and-eight at their own 40.

165

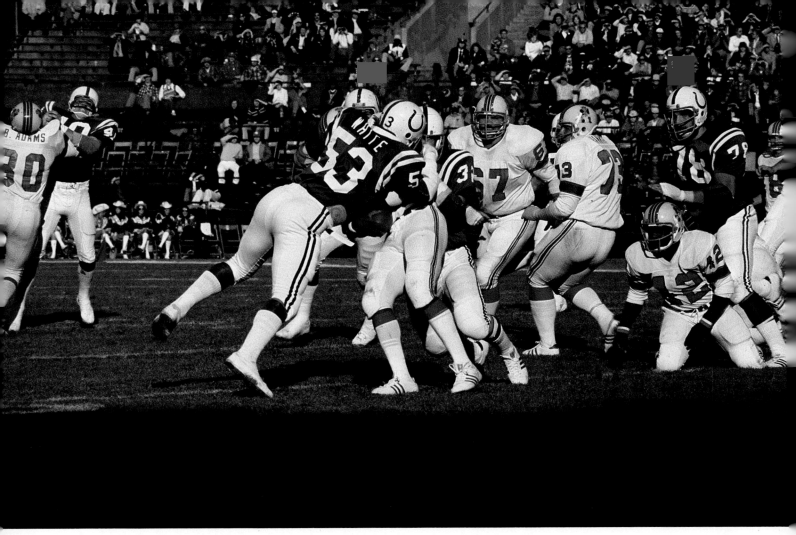

When asked to describe Stan White, head coach
Ted Marchibroda said"...he gives us a very
dependable and intelligent game." A seven year
veteran, Stan led the team in tackles in 1975 (119)
and 1976 (109) and holds a number of Club
defensive records.

Chester was in the clear deep but Jones overthrew him. It could have been six-points. After the game Chester talked about being open but added . . . "don't say nothing bad about the Boy Wonder". Before another training camp was to open Chester would be traded to the club that had originally owned him, the Raiders, the team the Colts had lost to on Christmas Eve, 1977.

The playoff with the Raiders was one of the most disappointing the Colts had ever known. It didn't end until 2:17 of the second overtime quarter, or after 77 minutes, 17 seconds had been played to obtain a verdict. Ken Stabler completed four passes to Dave Casper and three of them went for touchdowns, including a brilliant over-the-head catch which would have done justice to Willie Mays, and a ten yard catch in the left corner of the end-zone that ended the long, exciting afternoon. The score had been tied or changed hands eight times. It was an all-out shoot-out between Stabler and Jones, who was dropped six times by the Raiders' rapid rush.

Baltimore's fabled "Sack Pack", numbering John

Mike Curtis, Fred Miller and Ted Hendricks converge on a New England Patriot. Miller was an outstanding performer at defensive tackle for 10 seasons.

Dutton, Fred Cook, Joe Ehrmann and Mike Barnes, wasn't able to put the kind of pressure it wanted on Stabler but, the game, any way you look at it, than and now, rates as a football masterpiece. It was one of those rare occasions where neither team lost but only one could win.

The Colts, under Marchibroda, had gone three-for-three, meaning they had reached the playoffs in each of his first three seasons as head coach. It was a glittering attainment, even if they didn't win. But the second-guessers howled that he played too conservatively. This was a bum-rap. A coach has to stay with his philosophies. You don't devise a different type of game plan for playoffs than you do for what has been working effectively during the regualr season. Baltimore, in retrospect, had written another glorious football chapter.

It's a city and a team that has known the richness of triumph and the depths of despair that come with defeat. Through it all, the ups and downs, there had been a profound feeling of affection for professional football and a close identity that will always be the same, regardless of the names of the players on the field, the coach on the sideline, the general manager or the owner.

Baltimore will always take the Colts as something special — win, lose, Super Bowl qualifier or also-ran. They are indeed a way of life.

A very talented trio of linebackers (from l. to r.)
Ted Hendricks, Mike Curtis and Stan White.

168

Super fan Loudy Loudenslager thanks the Colts for honoring him and his wife Flo on December 9, 1973. Loudy has seen the Colts off and welcomed them home at the airport over 500 times and Flo never misses delivering a birthday cake for all members of the Colts' family. Looking on here are Jim Mutscheller (left) and Artie Donovan.

Glenn Doughty has given the Colts balance and consistency at wide receiver for the last three years. His 57 yard reception last year against the Patriots in the last and most crucial game of the season was the cataylist for the winning touchdown drive. Here he's out-running All-Pro safety Ken Houston and Gerard Williams of the Washington Redskins.

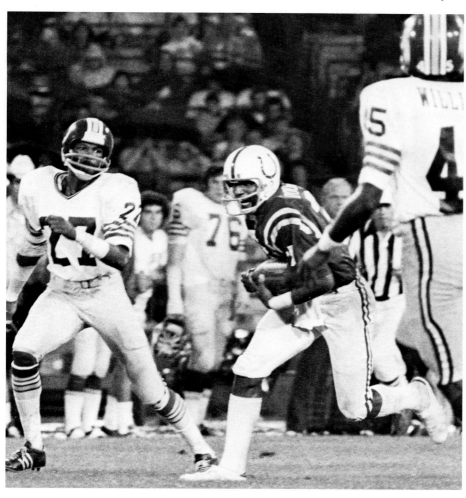

*Fred Cook puts the blast on Joe Namath as the
Colts walloped the Jets 52-19 in November, 1975.*

*Escorted by guard Ken Huff (62), Lydell Mitchell
takes off on an end sweep. Lydell is the only Colt
runningback who has rushed for over 1000 yards in
a season and he accomplished it three times (1975,
'76, '77).*

*One of the premier deep threats in the NFL, Roger
Carr gathers in this pass against the Bills in a 58-20
massacre for the Colts. Roger holds the club record
for the longest touchdown catch, a 90 yarder
against the Jets in 1975.*

*John Dutton led the Colts in quarterback sacks in
1975 (17) and 1976 (13) and has played an integral
part of the famed "Sack Pack."*

"The Sack Pack", (l. to r.) John Dutton (78), Joe Ehrmann (76), Mike Barnes (63) and Fred Cook (72).

*Mike Barnes prepares to lower the boom on the
Raiders' Ken Stabler.*

*Joe Ehrmann confronts MacArthur Lane of the
Kansas City Chiefs in a game won by the Colts in
1975, 28-14.*

Poetry in motion.

Between the two of them, they hold virtually every rushing record in the Colt record books. Here, Lenny Moore presents Lydell Mitchell with the ball after Lydell broke Lenny's all-time rushing mark of 5,174 yards on November 20, 1977. Lydell finished his Colt career with a total of 5,387 yards.

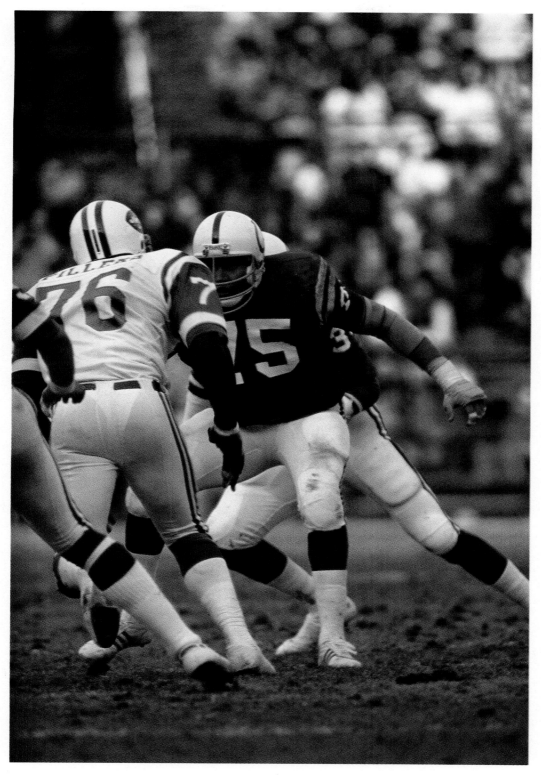

Ten year veteran George Kunz is considered one of the NFL's premier offensive tackles. He's been a five time All-Pro selection and has played in six Pro Bowl games.

On October 9, 1977 the Colts honored John Unitas
with a "day" to the delight and pleasure of 57,829 fans.

*Ed Thomas of the Colts' Band took this shot of the
1978 edition of the Baltimore Colts Marching Band
and Cheerleaders. Quite a change from 1947!*

Chuck Thompson has been doing the play by play announcing for Baltimore since the late 1940's. Nationally recognized and honored, Thompson lists his 1958 broadcast of the Colts-Giants sudden death championship game as one of his most memorable assignments.

No man has been with the Colts longer than Fred Schubach, who started with the team in 1953 as an equipment manger and ultimately became the chief of player personnel and scouting. Schubach spent his early boyhood with the Philadelphia Eagles, where his father was in charge of equipment.

A front office combination, Ernie Accorsi, assistant general manager, and Dick Szymanski, general manager, consult a file prior to the 1977 college draft.

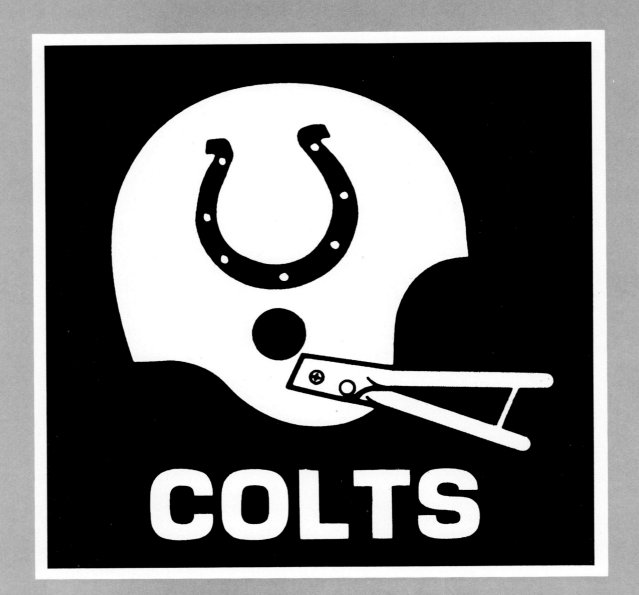

CHAPTER NINE
FOND MEMORIES

Pro football teams mean lots of things to different people.

To the millionaire owners, they are a vehicle to make money and satisfy egos and draw attention when they show up for lunch at the country club.

To the players and coaches, they provide a handsome income.

To the sports writers, they are something to write about.

To the fans, they are a vicarious way to gather thrills they wouldn't otherwise have.

The Baltimore Colts afford a montage of treasured memories, and the creation of enduring personal friendships that have lasted long after the scores of long-ago games have faded away like curling smoke escaping from a chimney in an old house by the side of the road.

Merely mentioning a name or a place triggers an immediate recollection:

Like Arthur Donovan...

He reported as a rookie in 1950 for a contract of $4,500 and played like he was being paid a million. His arrival was three days late because his father discouraged him. "Those big guys will kill him", his father warned his mother. The best he ever made at Boston College was second team All-New England but he was four times All-Pro, played in five Pro Bowls and was the first Colt to be enshrined in the Hall of Fame.

Like Pleasanton, Calif...

In 1949, our first trip ever with the Colts, they stopped at the Old Hearst Ranch between playing the San Francisco 49ers and Los Angeles Dons. Newspaper stories had to be taken to nearby Livermore, to a railroad telegraph station, where they were transmitted by Morse code. The old man wearing the green eye-shade would look at Jim Ellis of *The Evening Sun* and this reporter and say, "Another ball game today, boys?" Then he'd da-da-dit-dit the report of a bunch of over-grown kids perspiring on a grass field 3,000 miles from Baltimore.

Like Lamar Davis...

He was aptly nicknamed "Racehorse" and he went both ways for the Colts, offensive end, defensive halfback and also returned punts and kickoffs. He averaged 54 minutes a game in 1948 and weighed only 172-pounds. Now living in his native St. Simons Island, Ga., he weighs 240 and says, "I've enjoyed every pound of it".

Like New York...

The first time we went there as a publicity man, in 1955, we were uncertain how we would deal with the likes of such renowned columnists as Arthur Daley, Red Smith, Jimmy Powers and Dan Parker. To get even one of them to write a kind word about the Colts would make the trip worthwhile. But Daley, Smith and Powers used some of the column ideas we suggested and it felt to us like the Colts had scored a victory even before the game was played.

Like Claude (Buddy) Young...

A brilliant runner. He knew what it was to be a member of a minority, only 5-foot -4, but he made huge men respect him. Trainer Eddie Block referred to him as a "Little Giant". We laughed with each other and cried together. Knowing him made us a better human being, we prefer to believe.

Like Westminster, Md...

Those happy, busy days of training camp in the mid 1950s. The time Alex Sandusky put a ground-hog he had just shot in the bed of Art Donovan and we arranged to have his roommate, Art Spinney, turn on a wire recorder to get the reaction when he pulled down the covers and saw the "trophy". And then the night Madison (Buzz) Nutter got a key to the press room and stole all the beer that was being iced for the sports writers' pizza party.

Like Madison, Wis...

Seeing the restaurant, owned by Bob Lesk, where Alan (The Horse) Ameche left his Heisman Trophy on display. A great player and individual, Ameche never got puffed up with his own importance and didn't think it was at all unusual to let his friend have loan of the most prestigious award in college football. Madison also was where we met Roundy Coughlin, a sports writer, who was almost illiterate. He had trained for the business by cutting grass in the city square. So he always referred to himself as the "old lawn mower pusher". He wrote columns lacking in punctuation, continuity and grammatical construction but they were so different he was the most widely read writer in the area.

Like Lenny Moore...

The greatest natural talent these eyes have ever seen. He came up the hard way, living across a narrow lane in Reading, Pa., with garages facing the other side. The morning the Colts drafted him in 1956, coach Weeb Ewbank asked us to call State College, Pa., to try to get head coach Rip Engle and, if not Engle, then assistant Joe Paterno, who said, "Tell the Colts they're crazy if they don't take him. He can run out of the backfield and even play defense". Four times All-Pro, six Pro Bowls and enshrinment in the Hall of Fame.

Like Tulsa, Okla...

It was 1954 and the Colts' Buddy Young and John Latner of the Steelers put on a dazzling show of running in an exhibition game. Owner Art Rooney of the Steelers said Young was the most entertaining performer he had ever seen on a football field. We used the day of the game to hitch-hike to Claremore, Okla., to visit the shrine of that old cowboy philosopher, Will Rogers.

Like Eddie King...

A handsome middle guard with a square jaw and deeply religious. He went on to become the comptroller of the Boston Museum of Science, the much decorated Director of the Massachusetts Port Authority and, then, in 1978, a candidate for governor. Not a bad place to find a former interior lineman.

Like Palo Alto...

After curfew in back of the hotel, we had the car motor running, the lights out and then Gino Marchetti, Bill Pellington and Art Spinney, with a reporter driving, headed for a saloon owned by linebacker Marv Matuszak in Redwood City. It was an unforgettable night. We even tap-danced on the bar at closing time and the manager was angry. He said if we persisted in doing that he would have to charge an entertainment tax.

Like Dan Edwards...

He paid Maryland the all-time compliment when he said, "I've been all over the country and I live in Texas, which is supposed to be the greatest of all-states, but I never saw any place with the natural beauty of Maryland." Another time at the Sanoma Mission Inn, north of San Francisco, he quipped, "All you can do in this place is sit in a rocking chair and spit in the fire place."

Like Cameron Snyder...

A newspaper rival but a dear friend. We'd fight for each other in time of trouble. He had been a guard a Drexel Tech, in the late 1930s, when it was a top college team in the East, but we once beat him in a contest kicking field goals at the University of Chicago Stadium, only 40-yards away from where the early experiments were conducted on the development of the atom bomb. You could argue with him, trade insults but you knew you were with a beautiful human being.

Like Hershey, Pa...

This was where the Colts once played the Eagles a mid-summer exhibition game. It was fun. The beer lovers from Baltimore and Philadelphia always seemed to congregate for a drink-in and then the fights started, including a water battle with the field's sprinkling system as each side fought for control of the hose. It was better than the game.

Like Raymond Berry...

He was considered so eccentric the veteran players shook their heads in wonderment. He carried his own scale on road trips, wore blinders so he could sleep during daylight hours and even had a pair of sun glasses made so he could wear them on his helmet when the Colts played in Los Angeles Memorial Coliseum and had to cope with the setting sun "hanging" on the rim of the stadium. Totally dedicated and a genuine, considerate man. He made All-Pro three times, played in six Pro Bowls and was voted into the Hall of Fame.

Like Lubbock, Tex...

The Colts played the Chicago Cardinals an exhibition in 1953 and the visiting publicity man, Eddie McGuire, became somewhat confused. He went to Amarillo instead but recovered in time to make the kickoff. Maybe he knew that Lubbock was "dry" at the time and the only way to get a drink was to bribe the bellhop.

Like Ray (Wrong Way) Pelfrey...

A talented receiver and punter, he was a free spirit who enjoyed lining up players in training camp, putting lather on their faces and giving them shaves. He used to say, "I hope the coach doesn't put me on vanilla waifers". Pelfrey later wrote an excellent book on end play and now teaches a course in the proper techniques of punting.

Like Santa Barbara, Calif...

The Colts all went fishing in the blue Pacific. Gerald (Heap) Petersen, a 300-pound plus tackle, got sea sick on the boat and then that night had a few exotic drinks to forget his misery. He got sick all over again, tumbled in the bath-tub and even Artie Donovan couldn't lift him out. He slept the night away.

Like Willie (The Rooter) Andrews...

One of the most avid fans the Colts ever had. He even missed a car payment so he could travel to a road game and the vehicle was repossessed. Willie didn't care. He made paper-mache horses heads that he wore around Memorial Stadium and even led the "Gimme a C" cheer over the public address system. He died suddenly and Colts' players and executives served as his pall-bearers.

Like Hollywood...

Art Donovan, Sisto Averno and Y.A. Tittle wanted to go for a swim. It was at night, after curfew and they were confined to their hotel rooms. So they closed the stall-doors on the shower room, filled up the tub and let it rise. They jumped over the top but the three of them displaced so much water it spilled down on the floor and flooded the place, including the guest room underneath.

Like Art Spinney...

The kind of a man with the character and tenacity to always be a winner. He meant much to the Colts and was highly respected, on and off the field. One of our closest friends and because of that he was often accused of giving us exclusive stories, an allegation which was sometimes true.

Like Green Bay, Wis...

Where the priest at Sunday Mass talked about saving your soul but also the importance of the Packers beating the Colts that afternoon. A friendly community which has given much in legend and lore to the National Football League. You can feel the tradition put there by Lambeau and Lombardi.

Like Hurst Loudenslager...

A fanatical Colt follower who shows up at the airport to see the team "off" and is there at whatever hour it returns in the early morning, always playing the Colts' song on his tape recorder. There isn't anything he wouldn't do for a Colt player. One of his prized possessions is a bronzed athletic supporter worn by Gino Marchetti.

Like Dallas...

It was there in 1959 when we first met Lamar Hunt, father of the then infant, or still to be born American Football League. We were impressed with his love of the game and told one and all he would be successful in starting a new league that battled the established NFL for a foothold. The sport is better because of his determined desires.

Like Alex Hawkins...

A perpetual fun-seeker. he once escaped out of a hotel in San Francisco, after bed-check, by jumping from the second floor to a sandpile that just happened to be there for construction purposes. He got caught and was fined $500 by Coach Weeb Ewbank. Alex said he would just as soon pay double if he didn't have to listen to the coach's lecture. "When you dance you gotta pay the fiddler," reasoned Hawkins. Another time he offered to wager Bobby Boyd $1,000 he would ride naked on horseback from the Golden Arm Restaurant to Sweeney's in Waverly. Boyd wouldn't take the bet. He was wise. "The Hawk" would have done it.

Like Chicago...

The night Jerry Sheridan, a friend of Art Donovan's, took Art, Dick Barwegen, publicitor Sam Banks and a sports writer to a party at the Drake Hotel and the host, an oilman from St. Louis, whose name was Jimmy Dolan, said, "Boys, order whatever you want and just sign the tab." All of us left four hours later carrying a beer in each hand and a bottle in each coat pocket as we headed for the lobby to catch a cab.

Like Bert Rechichar...

A great football player who talked so tough he never had to back it up, but, in reality, is a kind, soft-hearted soul who would do anything for a friend. We asked him one time about a teammate at Tennessee named, Hank Lauricella, and he answered, "Yeah, I made that----." Rechichar was such an all-consummate player he went both ways in college during a two-platoon era. He kicked a world record field goal of 56 yards and later, when he introduced his friend Tom Keane, merely said, "This is the — — who held the ball."

Like San Francisco...

Visits there always meant going out with one of the most whimsical sports writers in the country, Prescott Sullivan of *The Examiner*. He never took himself seriously. His automobile was packed with old race track and football game programs, golf clubs, boxes of cigars, sweaters, jackets, caps, rain coats and debris. We asked him if the report was true there was a nest of mice living in the back seat under all that clutter. "I'm not sure, but it's some kind of wild-life", he answered. Another time an inquiry was made about how many times he had been married. He had that twinkle of mischief in his eyes and said, "I haven't checked with my computer lately."

Like Dick Szymanski...

He was ready to sign his first contract with the Colts in 1955. He agreed to terms, had pen in hand but looked at general manager Don Kellett and said, "I can't do it. I'm playing in a CYO basketball league and if we win our league we might have to forfeit if it's found out I signed in pro football." So Kellett told him to keep the contract and send it to him after the basketball season was over. A truly great player at either cener or linebacker. He has been only one way since the day he arrived...a decent and honorable individual. He has never been known to forget old friends.

Like Lake Placid, N.Y....

We were on our honeymoon but checked *The New York Times* after the Giants opened the season in Dallas against the Texans in 1952. The story said only 15,000 had watched the Cotton Bowl opener. We knew then that the Texans' team which had been transferred there from New York, nee Yanks, might now be making a U-turn back to Baltimore. It happened just that way. The honeymoon has been lasting.

PUBLISHER'S NOTE

We would like to express our deep appreciation to the Baltimore Colts organization and specifically to Mr. Ernie Accorsi, Assistant General Manager, Mr. Jim Husbands Director of Public Relations, and Mrs. Marge Blatt, Asst. Director of Public Relations, for their encouragement, time and help. Without their eager assistance, this book would not have been possible.

Our thanks, too, go to Mr. Joe Horrigan, Curator of the Pro Football Hall of Fame, who is always more than willing to help out with that "hard-to-find" photograph or piece of information. He is a talent all unto his own and we are most appreciative.

Jordan & Company
October, 1978